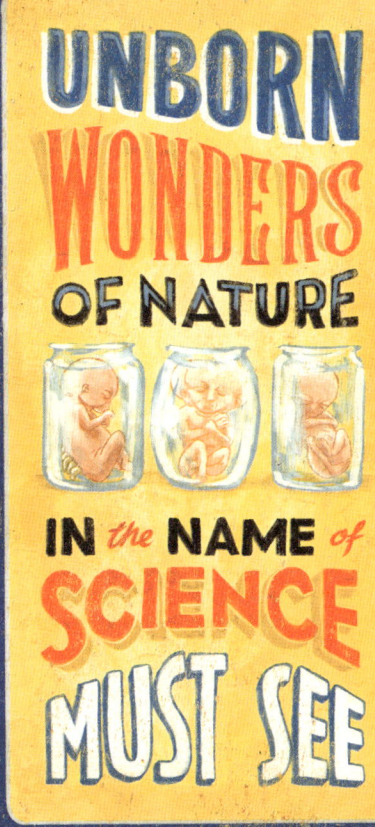

## GUILLERMO DEL TORO'S
# NIGHTMARE ALLEY

WRITTEN BY
**GINA McINTYRE**

FOREWORD BY
**GUILLERMO DEL TORO**

**TITAN BOOKS**
LONDON

# CONTENTS

### CHAPTER ONE
## THE FOOL
~ 10 ~

### CHAPTER TWO
## THE MAJOR ARCANA
~ 24 ~

### CHAPTER THREE
## THE WORLD
~ 64 ~

### CHAPTER FOUR
## RESURRECTION OF THE DEAD
~ 106 ~

### CHAPTER FIVE
## THE HANGED MAN
~ 142 ~

# FOREWORD
## A NIGHTMARE IN THE MAKING

**The price tag on the American dream is always a nightmare. Many writers and artists know this: Edward Hopper, George Bellows, James M. Cain, Raymond Chandler, Nathanael West, and, most certainly, William Lindsay Gresham.**

The soft underbelly of the winner mentality and the delicate betrayal of spirituality become evident in the machinations of Stanton Carlisle in Gresham's brilliant novel *Nightmare Alley*. Stanton is the "modern man"—the result of the tectonic clash of the material world (dough, dames, and darkness) and the sublime (loss, spirituality, and redemption). And in him we can see the downfall of us all. In Gresham's book, the carnival is a microcosm of the universe—it exists on the outskirts of paradise and tries to simulate it with garish colors and bright lights. The city is a trap: all illusion and sheen, but empty and full of darkness on the margins of its neon-lit streets.

These were virtues evident to both Kim Morgan and myself in the work of Gresham. We wanted to immerse ourselves not in the clichés of noir but in the compulsion that grasped America as it transitioned from the pastoral dream to the urban nightmare.

The quest proved phenomenal. The film took three years to make and encountered every difficulty imaginable. We wanted to make a lush, detailed film that looked like it had been made with three times its budget, and we wanted to combine modern, cutting-edge techniques with the "invisible" filmmaking elegance of classic cinema.

And, to make it harder, we ended up doing it during a pandemic.

I intended to render in color the "mid-tones" by art directing the use of greens and reds the way the studio-era masters would do in black and white films. This much I had learned whilst going through a brief apprenticeship with Gabriel Figueroa, the great Mexican cinematographer and contemporary of Gregg Toland: He showed me how olive greens or crimson reds render shades of black or grey that still hold enough "information" visually. He also showed me how he was able to affect the green of the trees or the contrast in a cloudy sky with green or red filters.

I was determined to do classic cross-lighting with our cinematographer, Dan Laustsen, and to photograph our colorful world using the "studio lighting" approach and saturated blacks. Together, we also decided to lower the ceilings of our sets so they were very close to our actors' heads, in order to be able to include them in low, wide-angle, depth-of-field-friendly compositions and staging.

As we entered the carnival portion of the shoot, I decided to view dailies in black and white, using the color settings on my laptop screen. It was my hope to allow the movie to decide its final shade during the postproduction process. This proved arduous and tortuous—but worthwhile in keeping the strong visual language alive.

Production designer Tamara Deverell and set decorator Shane Vieau helped me make sure that Stanton was always either in an alley (sets were built to create that illusion), trapped within a circle (the geek pit), or reflected in a mirror (the illusion). And, as always, we were careful to use the color red very sparingly and precisely.

Costume designer Luis Sequeira and I went on a quest to try to make each character unique by dressing them in the diverse language of apparel that existed in the late '30s and early '40s in the USA—thus leather jackets, fedoras, pinstripe suits, and silk gowns had to stand side-by-side.

The preproduction and scouting took longer than they have on most projects I've ever tackled: We needed to find the perfect doorway, the perfect street, the perfect field for every frame.

And then came the casting: We not only managed to get a Cadillac actor for every single part in the script, but also found partners that deep-dived with us into this world and style—they brought humanity, precision, and care to every decision we made. And for me, personally, my partnership with Bradley Cooper became the singularity of a lifetime: a privilege and a marathon for excellence.

Stanton—and therefore Bradley—is on-screen 99 percent of the time, so "tracking" him emotionally was a must, and no decision was made lightly. Having Bradley as an accomplice in this was key to the endeavor.

No film has ever demanded more of me than this one. It surprised me and challenged me and my producing partner, J. Miles Dale, every hour, every day, for months and months in a row. And now, as I write these words, it is nearly finished—we are locking picture and getting ready for the final color grading, scoring, and mixing.

How will the film land? Who will embrace it? I have no idea. And that, I have learned, is the way one makes films: We make the unlikely ones, the ones that shine a beacon into our souls and guide us through the most brutal, unforgiving terrain—the ones that show us a new horizon.

I have tried with every film to reinvent myself in some basic way: *Pacific Rim* exists side by side with *Pan's Labyrinth*, and though they could not be any more different, they are nurtured by the same heart and degree of care. And now comes *Nightmare Alley*.

After *The Shape of Water*, the world took a dark turn, in my view. We all were exposed to the basest side of human nature, and *Nightmare Alley* reflects how I feel about what I experienced during such times—experiences I believe we all shared.

Our film is, I hope, a black diamond—one which holds our reflection in the sheen and polish of its surface.

Stare deep, stare long—and behold the Nightmare.

**Guillermo del Toro
September 2021**

**ABOVE** Guillermo del Toro (far left) directs stars (left to right) Ron Perlman, Bradley Cooper, Toni Collette, Rooney Mara, and Mark Povinelli.

# INTRODUCTION

William Lindsay Gresham was drinking with an old-time carny in late-1930s Spain when he heard a story that would haunt him for years to come. Then twenty-nine years old, Gresham had volunteered as a medical orderly in the Spanish Civil War, witnessing true horrors on the battlefield. Still, he was left shaken as his companion, a sergeant of medics, began to tell him about a gruesome carnival act: the geek show. In it, a bedraggled man would be thrown live chickens and snakes, which he would then pick up and dismember with his teeth. Fascinated and disturbed by the story, Gresham did not forget the notion of such men—the wretches who performed these acts were almost always poor and in the grips of addiction.

Years later, with the September 1946 publication of his groundbreaking, subversive novel *Nightmare Alley*, Gresham popularized the term "geek." This pitiable character plays a haunting central role in Gresham's lurid post-Depression story of the rise and fall of the opportunistic Stanton Carlisle, a wicked yet charismatic and troubled con man whose fate is inextricably bound up with that of a traveling carnival.

Critics hailed the book for its rich, hard-bitten vernacular and a compelling narrative centering on characters who dwell at the margins of society. Although it remained on the best-seller list for a year, Gresham's novel was also reviled in some quarters—its content deemed too risqué for conventional tastes. In the three decades that followed its release, the book was frequently censored, with Gresham's raw language softened for sensitive eyes—harsh passages such as "society dames with the clap, bankers that take it up the ass" were doctored to read "society dames with a dose, bankers that have fishy eyes."

Still, Gresham's evocative, Freudian thriller mesmerized generations of readers by compellingly manifesting many of its author's obsessions, including psychoanalysis, the tarot, mentalism, and the occult. Among the book's devotees was acclaimed writer-director Guillermo del Toro, who, after winning the Academy Award for his 2017 romantic fable *The Shape of Water*, chose to next adapt Gresham's story for the screen. "*Nightmare Alley* is one of the great 'underbelly of America' novels," says del Toro. "It chronicles the rise and fall of a liar, a hollow man who rises to the highest echelons of social life. What is beautiful about it is that it's full of magical, emotional, suspenseful, dark, human moments."

Since making his feature film debut with 1993's Spanish-language vampire tale *Cronos*, del Toro repeatedly has conjured visually stunning, magical stories that celebrate the beauty that can exist within darkness. In such films as *The Devil's Backbone* (2001), *Hellboy* (2004), *Pan's Labyrinth* (2006), and, of course, *The Shape of Water*, del Toro reveals the humanity of those too often perceived as "other"—monsters and demons, ghosts, an amphibious river god saved from extinction by a mute janitor.

Yet if *The Shape of Water* was a fairy tale extolling the empowering nature of love, *Nightmare Alley* arrives as its sinister, blackhearted corollary. Love is an emotion protagonist Stanton Carlisle seeks but perhaps will never understand—he is ambitious to a fault and permanently, inevitably unsatisfied. Fate isn't always kind to such men, and just as in Gresham's novel, Stan's sinful pride presages an unimaginable downfall. "I was very much interested in a tale about destiny and humanity, about a character that could change his life," says del Toro. "He has people that believe in him, people that love him, people that trust him. Yet his drive, his own hubris, is so strong that it becomes destiny.

"There are only two stories that are worth telling in any form: a character that wins everything and a character that loses everything," he adds. "This is the latter."

**ABOVE** Lilith Ritter (Cate Blanchett) proves to be a powerful force in the life of Stanton Carlisle (Bradley Cooper).
**OPPOSITE** The role required Cooper (pictured) to become comfortable with the accessories of the period, such as Stan's fedora.

## CHAPTER ONE
# THE FOOL

*Who walks in motley, with his eyes closed, over a precipice at the end of the world.*

Guillermo del Toro first became acquainted with Gresham's story when he was still a young filmmaker in Mexico. While shooting his feature debut *Cronos*, the first-time director and actor Ron Perlman struck up a lifelong friendship spurred by their shared love of horror. During their conversations, Perlman brought up his abiding affection for the 1947 movie adaptation of *Nightmare Alley* starring Tyrone Power as Stan. Del Toro had never seen the hard-to-find film but was intrigued by its premise: A duplicitous con man makes his fortune by repurposing a carnival act into a lucrative mentalism career only to lose everything after an ill-advised scam goes wrong.

*Nightmare Alley* was something of an oddity in both Power's career and in the annals of Hollywood. 20th Century Fox chairman and Hollywood power broker Darryl F. Zanuck had bought the rights to Gresham's book at the urging of famed Vaudeville performer-turned-producer George Jessel, but once Zanuck read the novel, he developed grave concerns about the material. He quickly realized that any adaptation would need to downplay or omit the source material's most salacious aspects.

Power, however, was excited by the opportunity to delve into Stanton Carlisle's psychology. At the time, the actor was best known for swashbuckling adventures and sweeping romances, such as 1946's Oscar-nominated drama *The Razor's Edge*, in which he played a World War I pilot who undertakes a search for spiritual meaning. Eager to demonstrate his range, he lobbied for the chance to play Stan, a role that would serve as an impressive showcase for his talents.

The idea of Power playing a grifter who gets a terrible comeuppance was not especially appealing to Zanuck, who was reluctant to cast his affable leading man as such a morally compromised character. Still, given Power's enthusiasm for the role, Zanuck eventually capitulated. Power recruited his *Razor's Edge* director, Edmund Goulding, and *Nightmare Alley* was soon underway.

When the movie opened, Zanuck's lack of faith in the project became evident. The powerful mogul oversaw a release strategy that all but ensured the film would have minimal impact. Although Power delivered a masterful starring turn, *Nightmare Alley* was pulled from theaters early. While Power successfully resumed his career, appearing in such films as 1951's *Rawhide* and 1957's *The Sun Also Rises*, *Nightmare Alley* remained a fascinating oddity in his career, even if it was deemed a failure at the time. The film was not entirely forgotten, however, and later thrived on the margins thanks to television showings. It became a coveted cult movie—one people talked about whether they'd seen it or not. Adding to its cult status, *Nightmare Alley* didn't reach the home video market until 2005 because of legal wrangling between Jessel's estate and the studio.

Despite the obscure nature of the 1947 film, Perlman and del Toro tracked down a copy while *Cronos* was in postproduction, and the writer-director immediately sparked to the story, which dovetailed with many of his interests. "I have been investigating magic and carnival life all my life," he says. "I'm friends with magicians, and I, myself, am a terrible, terrible, terrible, nonperforming magician. But I admire the craft of mentalism and all the trimmings that come with mind reading, or that simulate a mind reading."

After watching the film, del Toro next obtained a copy of Gresham's novel to better ground himself in Stanton's story. Enamored with Gresham's work, he set his sights on adapting the book. "The funny thing is that it came from Ron and I talking about the fact that the two things I wanted to do when I was young were noir and horror," del Toro says. "That's all I wanted to do." As he researched the rights to both the 1946 novel and the 1947 movie, however, he was told there were ongoing legal issues entangling the properties.

 **ABOVE** Concept image depicting Nightmare Alley, a narrow, brick-lined space that Stan visits in his dreams; the film's production design team constructed an actual brick alley for the movie, and several sequences were filmed using that set. Guillermo del Toro, however, ultimately chose not to include those scenes in the final cut of the film.
**RIGHT** Concept art that shows drunken carnival performer Pete Krumbein napping in the area beneath the stage where his wife, Zeena the Seer, performs.

# A NIGHTMARE RESURRECTED

**When del Toro at last returned to the idea of adapting *Nightmare Alley*,** he was in a vastly different place in his career. Rather than being a promising newcomer, he was coming off his first best picture Oscar win for *The Shape of Water* with enough clout to get any number of dream projects made. Still, he didn't necessarily see *Nightmare Alley* as a viable endeavor, suspecting that the subject matter was too dark, the story too sprawling, and the budget required too high for any major studio to consider financing a new adaptation.

Nevertheless, del Toro decided to begin work on a new *Nightmare Alley* script after he and Kim Morgan, also an admirer of the novel, discussed their shared interest in the material. A longtime film and culture writer whose work has appeared in the Criterion Collection, The New Beverly Cinema, *Sight & Sound*, *Filmmaker Magazine*, and the *Los Angeles Review of Books*, Morgan had similarly been taken by not just the novel, but also the world it presented and Gresham himself. They

**TOP** Concept art for the carnival that Stan joins at the beginning of *Nightmare Alley*.
**ABOVE** Bradley Cooper and Rooney Mara flank filmmaker Guillermo del Toro as he reviews a scene set in Buffalo, New York.
**OPPOSITE** Concept art depicting the exterior of the Copacabana, the chic Buffalo nightclub where Stanton will become a star performer.

decided to collaborate on adapting the book as a joint writing exercise. "We didn't want to remake the original film as much as we wanted to try to reapproach the novel," says del Toro.

Together, they re-read their copies of *Nightmare Alley*, and re-read them again, underlining passages that struck them as especially dynamic or profound. In the process, they became even more intrigued by Gresham and the similarities they discovered between the writer and his protagonist: "He is one of the main reasons why we undertook the movie," says del Toro. "He's Stan."

The details might be different, but it's true that the substance of Gresham's life does mirror that of his fictional alter ego. He became interested in carnival life early, after moving to New York as a boy and seeing a sideshow at Coney Island. Later, in his teen years, he spent time with the performers, learning the intricacies of their world. "He says actually the [carnies] were some of the few people who saw him for who he was, good and bad," del Toro says. "He was very moved by that." He used his insider knowledge—as well as the fateful conversation in Spain—as the basis for both *Nightmare Alley* and 1953's behind-the-scenes tell-all *Monster Midway: An Uninhibited Look at the Glittering World of the Carny*.

Prone to violence and alcoholism, Gresham unquestionably wrestled with his own baser nature. Financial instability, along with his abusive outbursts and drinking, plagued his marriage to his wife, poet Joy Davidman, with whom he had two sons. After their divorce, Gresham married her first cousin, with whom he'd been having an affair. Davidman embarked on a second marriage of her own to the *Chronicles of Narnia* author and respected academic C. S. Lewis in 1956, though their union was short-lived. She died of cancer four years later at the age of 45.

As Gresham continued to write—penning, among other things, a biography of Harry Houdini, and another novel, *Limbo Tower*, as well as a book on bodybuilding—he aligned himself with various philosophies in hopes of finding enlightenment, only to eventually drop them in favor of something new.

"I became so fascinated by him and all of the different things that he would cycle through or keep hold of," Morgan says. "Among these, there was the tarot, Freudian psychoanalysis. There was Christianity. He was in Alcoholics Anonymous. He was involved in Dianetics but didn't stay with that. These seemed to me all of the ways he was searching—for enlightenment, for a deeper understanding of the world and beyond, and for searching inside himself. But sometimes looking into yourself can be disturbing."

Adds del Toro: "Gresham was a seeker, the Fool in the tarot cards. He wanted to find God or divinity or fate, something larger than man. But he always ended up finding the abyss."

Ultimately, whatever Gresham was seeking might have eluded him. His own story ended in 1962 when, after receiving a cancer diagnosis, he took his own life. He was fifty-three years old. "He is a guy who had, I thought, a hard time reconciling the spiritual dimension with the brutal vulgarity of the world," says del Toro. "That was his quest. But we were fascinated by the darker side of his own journey to find who he was as a human and a man [as well as] the spiritual symbolic dimension, the sexual dimension, the fact that he investigates masculinity and femininity as spiritual energies in *Nightmare Alley*. It's an interesting mélange of things."

# HISTORY LESSONS

At the same time that del Toro and Morgan were studying Gresham, they were also undertaking historical research in an effort to accurately position their story in time. The film opens in 1939, coinciding with the outbreak of World War II, a uniquely dangerous and chaotic period that would come to reshape virtually every facet of life for millions of people around the globe. When the story concludes, it's 1941, the year the U.S. is drawn into the fight. A new decade has dawned, one that feels like a seismic first step into a future clouded by the terrible conflict.

As they dived back into the past, del Toro and Morgan developed a keen ear for the slang of the era and the patter of the speech, taking cues and, in some cases, specific lines from Gresham's novel. "He has an incredible ear for the vernacular," del Toro says. "There are certain idioms he uses—'He looked real kippy,' or 'It's all eggs and coffee,' which is 'Everything's fine.' But you've got to be very careful that you don't end up with movie dialogue from the '30s. That's the trick, that you don't end up saying, 'Look at the gams on that tomato!'"

Films from the early 1930s, however, did provide additional inspiration for del Toro and Morgan. In particular, del Toro studied Tod Browning's 1933 drama *Fast Workers*, about a pair of welders who become romantic rivals, to try to capture the rhythm of its language. Morgan loved William Wellman's 1933 *Heroes for Sale*, about a war veteran who returns home addicted to morphine—this and *Fast Workers* were made before Hollywood instituted the Hays Code to ensure that studio films adhered to strict moral guidelines. Watching those and other pre-Code films, including Wellman's *Wild Boys of the Road* and *Other Men's Women*, George Hill's *The Big House*, and more also helped del Toro determine how he wanted to shoot *Nightmare Alley*.

"I studied as much as possible William Wellman, William Wyler, Mervyn LeRoy—the classical filmmakers," del Toro says. "And, of course, all Otto Preminger's 20th Century Fox noirs like *Fallen Angel* and *Where the Sidewalk Ends*. I love how the craft was unobtrusive and beautiful and realistic, like when you watch pre-Code Wellman. I was struck by how harsh he could be and how unflinching his camera could be—and how mobile his camera could be without being showy, like in *Other Men's Women*, where the camera can be mounted on train tracks or wagons or glide along. For *Nightmare Alley*, I wanted to try not to stylize things too much and keep them at that level with long, single unbroken master takes that were not self-serving but discreet and well designed."

That approach was well suited for a story where, although the supernatural is certainly thematically present, it isn't real. Notably, *Nightmare Alley* includes no ghosts or creatures of any kind, but the filmmaker insists that in no way did that aspect of the storytelling feel like a departure for him. "I believe that spirituality and reality are of a piece," del Toro says. "There is no supernatural, but there is an eeriness and a heightened sense of destiny coming from us. The difference was that this movie needed to be grounded on a very, very palpable everyday reality that felt lived in and quotidian, that the characters were real. Even if the story had heightened elements, the characters needed to remain real and the world needed to remain real."

**OPPOSITE** A page from Guillermo del Toro's personal notebooks shows an early concept for a carnival attraction. **BELOW** Storyboards by concept artist Guy Davis for a scene in which workers pack up the carnival before it moves on to a new town. Del Toro calls Davis "a fabulous artist and frequent collaborator."

- El ayudante del vampiro se corta el cuello sobre la tierra en una de las cajas y de ahí sale Manú
- Los pecados en el funhouse deben de ser profecía de lo que le va a pasar a Stan en la película. y el TAROT igual (usan símbolos sin dinero?)
- Si Zeena pierde la libreta, entonces Molly debería de destruirla e irse, dejando a Stan sin salida alguna (NO ESCRIBIÓ el código) ni nadie que lo quiera ayudar. A la chimenea.

"FUNHOUSE STAN"

- La mujer araña que se quedó así por desobedecer a sus padres. Clem carga un bote.
- Clem tiene lentes negros y UN guante de cuero
- Pete sin barba completa / con goatee sucio.
- El vampiro silueteado contra la ola que sale del océano. Agarrado de un mástil en tormenta.
- trepa por el techo con la alas como murciélago.
- The CURVE of the funhouse is also a cycle - the eternal return - NEVER ENDING loop between heaven and hell. Visualize the curve.

# UNDERSTANDING STAN

**Of the previous feature films del Toro has directed, many center on outwardly monstrous creatures who nevertheless make for admirable protagonists—they are monsters who are easy to love. In *Cronos*, it's a kindly grandfather transformed into a vampire; in the two Hellboy movies, it's a surly half-demon with a powerful romantic streak; in *The Shape of Water*, it's Doug Jones's regal amphibian man. In that sense, *Nightmare Alley* feels like a radical departure. Here, with his blue eyes and broad shoulders, Stanton Carlisle might be physically handsome, but his defining qualities—his selfishness, his amorality, the way he inflicts casual cruelties on the people around him—are morally repugnant.**

Yet as del Toro and Morgan were drafting the script, they often found it necessary to see the world through Stan's eyes, which made his decisions and the motivations behind them more relatable. "You can't help but find yourself relating to Stan at times—I did, at least—even though he can be despicable," Morgan says. "We all have our fears, and I felt that Stan was filled with a lot of fear. To get into his mindset was actually haunting at times—to be in that headspace, thinking of all the things back in his past. He's a very flawed, troubled human being who is trying to get through it, one who eventually tries to drown the demons with drink, but he also seems drawn to the abyss even as he seems to be running from it." Adds del Toro: "Writing Stan for me is almost like writing and observing darkness."

Even among outcasts, Stan remains an outsider. When he wanders into the traveling carnival at the start of *Nightmare Alley*, he has almost nothing. Desperate for a job and a hot meal, he gets himself hired as a workhand—an unexpected turn of events that sets him on a path toward his destiny. Although the professional carnies regard him with hostility and suspicion—especially intimidating boss Clem—Stan ingratiates himself into their ranks.

Before long, he embarks on a relationship with psychic Zeena and befriends her ailing husband, Pete. All the while, he's secretly captivated by performer Molly, whose electrifying stage act makes her something of a rising star within the carnival.

"I understand Stan in the sense that a storyteller spends most of his or her life watching and observing and absorbing—but [with the purpose of telling] a story," del Toro says. "Stan does it to manipulate. But I understand the essential loneliness of the storyteller. You are outside of society, looking in. If you're part of the banquet, you cannot see it very clearly. But if you're outside, sometimes you can, and Stan is."

After an unfortunate death paves the way for Stan to steal the mentalism act that once brought Zeena and Pete fame and fortune, he and Molly leave the small-town traveling circus life behind. Together, they head for the bright lights of the New York city of Buffalo, where they, too, enjoy all the trappings of wealth and success. But a fateful encounter with a mysterious psychiatrist, Lilith Ritter, marks the beginning of a new obsession for Stan. With Lilith's help, he sets about using the skills he's acquired to defraud powerful local magnate Ezra Grindle, a man desperate to be forgiven for a terrible act in his past.

Blind to the peril surrounding him, Stan makes a grave series of miscalculations with unimaginable consequences. In a moment, all is lost. "That's one of the things that happens in the literature we love," del Toro says. "Certainly, it happens in the novels of James M. Cain. When you read

*Mildred Pierce, Double Indemnity*—a lifetime of hard work can evaporate in one minute by one action. And that was one thing that I thought was very interesting in writing Stan—he thinks he's going to get out of this one night with some money. Will he call it a day? Maybe not, but he thinks he could. Some people lie and convince themselves that that's the truth."

Yet what motivates Stanton Carlisle isn't just arrogance and greed—it's also fear. "You can read a lot into Stan," Morgan says. "He's a great manipulator, he's good-looking. He's all these things, but deep down he seems very insecure to me. He's so haunted by the geek. Deep down, there's that fear in him—I could be *there*."

Nor is he the only character in the film capable of savagery. "We wanted to see terrible things," says del Toro. "Little treacheries in Zeena. We wanted to see darkness in Clem. We wanted Stan to have good and bad because at the end of the day, the only chance we have is if we make peace with the darkness that is part of us and keep it in check. It's not a black-and-white universe."

**OPPOSITE TOP LEFT** Bradley Cooper in costume as Stanton Carlisle discusses one of *Nightmare Alley*'s opening scenes with Guillermo del Toro (right), who is equipped with a face shield for safety.
**OPPOSITE TOP RIGHT** During the shoot, del Toro and Cooper were in constant communication, collaborating closely on every scene. "He and Guillermo were very much on top of every facet of the film," says co-star Rooney Mara.
**ABOVE** Del Toro confers with (left to right) director of photography Dan Laustsen, Cooper, A camera and Steadicam operator Gilles Corbeil, VFX supervisor Greg Sigurdson, and writer Kim Morgan.
**PAGES 20–21** Facing pages from del Toro's personal notebooks depict an early concept for the outfit Stan would wear during his time as a professional mystic in Buffalo, New York.

- ⭕ Es el lenguaje visual del DESTINO del que NO puede escapar. Es el pozo del Geek, el dial de la radio, un ojo que lo vigila constantemente LA MIRADA DE DIOS.
- Grindle es su padre, Zeena es su madre.
- La clave es la transición entre el carnaval y la ciudad. NO USAR ROJO en la ciudad: Blanco, Negro, gris, dorado, verde.
- evitar el PURPURA o los VIOLETAS en la ciudad. NO usar nada hecho a mano en ningún lado: La madera y el arte deben de sentirse ensamblados y fríos. Solo en la casa de los Hunnington debe haber OLEOS y SOLO retratos. NO PAISAJES.
- TODOS los letreros en el carnaval son hechos a mano (LA TAPA ROJA del frasco). Buscar imperfecciones en el vidrio de los jarros de los pickled punks. Solo MOLLY en rojo.
- El mayor y Bruno son UNO solo. Fusión.
- Abrir con un iris y cerrar con un iris del ojo de Enoch al iris de inicio Stan se bate.
- Hay que asegurarse de CÓMO se fuman en CINE
- 👁 como símbolo del destino en la película: ENOCH, ZEENA, STAN, FUNHOUSE, el billete de a dólar; LA PIRÁMIDE QUE MIRA.
- Stan diseña una mesa que da golpes en madera. Molly da apoyo con un magneto en su anillo.
- Alguien toca los BLUES en la guitarra. Música debe incluir TIN PAN ALLEY y early COUNTRY music (godellia?) como contraste constante. Debe estar la simplicidad "FOLKSY" del país imaginario y la ominosa neurosis que subyace.
- Stan estrena el disfraz de REVERENDO al ir a buscar los datos del fallecimiento (BIBLIOTECA)

## GETTING THE GREEN LIGHT

After roughly six months, del Toro and Morgan completed their *Nightmare Alley* script. The pair submitted the screenplay to the executive team at Searchlight Pictures, which had released *The Shape of Water* to such acclaim. Despite del Toro's positive experiences with the studio, he still worried that they might not warm to the carnival tale, with its expansive scope and difficult ending. He and Morgan were pleasantly surprised by the enthusiastic reception the screenplay received, however. "They said, 'Okay, if you cast it strong, we will green-light it,'" del Toro recalls.

With that in mind, del Toro began to search for the right roster of gifted actors to fill out *Nightmare Alley*'s ensemble, while also assembling a strong behind-the-scenes creative team that included many of his *Shape of Water* collaborators: producer J. Miles Dale, cinematographer Dan Laustsen, and costume designer Luis Sequeira, among them.

"We wanted to art direct the film in colors that would result in the perfect mid-tones if we rendered the film in black and white," del Toro says. "Dan and I decided the film should be lit with classical cross-lighting but be able to go color or black and white at will. Once we were shooting the carnival portion, I started viewing dailies in black and white to check our concept. I secretly hoped we could use both stock looks in the film in a meaningful way. I started to seek that."

Given the film's strong focus on character, del Toro understood that the true success of the project would live and die with the actors he cast. Particularly important was nailing the casting of Stanton Carlisle, a character who appears in almost every scene in the film. "I knew I needed somebody that would be a deep-dive partner," del Toro says.

Fortunately, he found that and more in Bradley Cooper, the eight-time Academy Award–nominated writer-director-actor who would become a creative soul mate to del Toro and a producer on *Nightmare Alley*. "By now, we have something that I've never had, which is almost like an intestinal bypass that connects our guts at a very fundamental level," del Toro says. "I know how he's going to react before anything is said. And he knows me two beats ahead in the same way. There was an understanding of what was in the balance for the whole movie, not just this character. He understands the entire mosaic."

Together, del Toro, Cooper, and the rest of the cast and crew set out to explore a world of the recent past—one that also serves as a dark reflection of our present moment, full of discomfiting images, fear, betrayal, and deceit.

"The movie was gestated during the Trump era, and for me there was an undercurrent in the movie about lying—there's nobody lonelier than a liar," del Toro says. "The truth connects you. Lies isolate you, no matter how small they are, because you become the guardian of that. With a lie comes a whole reality, and when somebody lies for a living, what is the face of truth?"

**OPPOSITE** *Nightmare Alley* director of photography Dan Laustsen, who earned an Oscar nomination for *The Shape of Water*, his previous collaboration with del Toro.
**ABOVE** For the new thriller, del Toro (left) also reteamed with frequent producing partner J. Miles Dale (right).

## CHAPTER TWO
# THE MAJOR ARCANA

*The foundational cards in the tarot deck represent archetypes, symbolic figures, and situations of great significance.*

## STANTON CARLISLE
### BRADLEY COOPER

**Long before he stepped into the director's chair with his acclaimed 2018 remake of *A Star Is Born*, Bradley Cooper had established himself as one of his generation's most versatile talents.**

After a breakthrough role on the TV series *Alias*, Cooper went on to build a lengthy résumé featuring crowd-pleasing blockbusters including *The Hangover* (2009) and *Guardians of the Galaxy* (2014) as well as critically lauded dramas such as *Silver Linings Playbook* (2012), *American Hustle* (2013), and *American Sniper* (2014). He also earned rave reviews starring on Broadway and the West End as Joseph Merrick in Bernard Pomerance's play *The Elephant Man*—the story of the 19th century Englishman whose physical deformities landed him in a sideshow.

With *A Star Is Born*, Cooper delivered one of his most compelling performances yet as singer-songwriter Jackson Maine, whose struggles with alcoholism exact a heartbreaking toll. Not only that, but he also proved he's a gifted filmmaker with a unique eye capable of creating a visually compelling drama that is also emotionally powerful. The movie became a full-fledged cultural sensation and was nominated for eight Oscars, including best actor for Cooper and best picture. It ultimately took home one Academy Award for the hit song "Shallow," which Cooper performed with co-star Lady Gaga.

Cooper was in the thick of preparing for his follow-up, *Maestro*—about the romance between legendary American conductor Leonard Bernstein and his wife, Felicia—when Guillermo del Toro contacted him to discuss the role of Stanton Carlisle. "Stan is basically the incarnation of that Jungian maxim 'Until you make the unconscious conscious, it will direct your life and you will call it fate,'" explains del Toro. "I thought, *Who can track a character like that all the way to the final scene?* Before I met with Bradley the first time, I spoke with people who had worked with him who said that none of his choices were casual. I thought, okay, that is what I need because this movie needs to feel real with a character who is onscreen 99 percent of the time."

Despite his focus on *Maestro*, Cooper agreed to meet with del Toro, who visited the actor at his home. "I reaffirmed my commitment by going to his house, which is full of stairs," del Toro says. "And for me, stairs are like kryptonite for Superman. I went up two or three flights to meet him on the terrace. Then he says, 'Do you mind meeting next to the pool?' Which is another flight of stairs."

Scaling the heights of Cooper's residence turned out to be worth it. In Cooper, del Toro found not only his perfect leading man, but an ideal artistic collaborator who became integral to realizing the filmmaker's vision for *Nightmare Alley*. "What Bradley Cooper brings is very moving," del Toro says. "He has all the goodness and the physical beauty and an innate grace to show what Stan could be. And at the same time, he brings the skill of one of the most superb actors of his generation to create a character of deep, deep darkness."

When he met with Cooper, del Toro brought a copy of Gresham's *Monster Midway*, plus a book of photographs featuring 1930s Australian criminals, both vivid references for Stan's world. They

**PAGES 27–28** (clockwise from left) Stanton (Bradley Cooper) has few possessions when he arrives at the carnival; a dapper Stanton holds the white rabbit that once belonged to Pete Krumbein (David Strathairn); Stan pays a small fee to wash up in the bathroom at Zeena's carnival bungalow.
**OPPOSITE** Stan (Cooper) sweeps the floors near the cage where the carnival's geek (Paul Anderson, left) is forced to sleep on a bed of straw.
**BELOW** Stan (Cooper) makes a repair to Zeena's truck.
**RIGHT** A sketch by costume designer Luis Sequeira depicting Stan's look when he arrives at the carnival seeking work.

discussed the physicality that would be required for the role, and del Toro told Cooper he wanted him to learn to box to attain the right build, and the proper pugilistic mindset.

"Stan needed to be a boxer," del Toro says. "A character like Stan undoubtedly would exist in a world where physical altercations and hardship would be day-to-day. I told him, 'If you are able to physically survive day-to-day boxing and training, that's part of Stan's makeup for me.' He trained and boxed for weeks in a row, leading all the way to the shoot. I think he still thinks that was one of the keys to the character."

Another was Stan's voice. Finding the right pitch, intonation, and accent for each character he plays is always pivotal for Cooper, so after committing to star in *Nightmare Alley* in the summer of 2019, he started working with dialect coach Tim Monich to perfect Stan's speech patterns.

Stan's few possessions offered additional insight into the character—the most important being the watch that belonged to his late father, whose presence seems to loom over Stan like an inescapable shadow. Stan wears the cheap brass timepiece around his wrist, binding him to someone he seems to love and hate in equal measure. He also has a sketchbook that he carries with him, drawing in its pages the people and places he encounters.

"We tried to tell who he was through the few props that he possesses and the way that he carries himself in the carnival and the way he carries himself in the city," del Toro says. "He's a loner who observes and absorbs. That's the main characteristic, I think, of Stan."

Del Toro also felt that Cooper had a unique ability to gracefully wear the accoutrements of the period, particularly Stan's brown fedora. "This is going to sound very obsessive, but one of the things that I don't think contemporary actors handle well are props of

**THESE PAGES** Throughout *Nightmare Alley*, Stan is seen making pencil sketches of the people and places he encounters, recording his experiences like a visual diary. The black-and-white sketches were created by Canadian visual artist and educator Geordie Millar based on reference images provided by production designer Tamara Deverell and her team.

the period like the hat and wearing the clothes the right way," del Toro says. "Wearing the hat is a whole language, the way you grab it, the way you handle it. The props and the way Stan stands or moves or takes off his hat, I think we nailed all of that."

As del Toro and Cooper worked together to develop Stan's voice and bearing, they also began to bond on a deeper level, examining the entirety of the film together—in terms of both the story and the composition of certain scenes. Although del Toro has enjoyed long-running and fruitful artistic collaborations in his past with stars including Ron Perlman and Doug Jones, his rapport with Cooper was unique, informed by Cooper's own experience in the director's chair.

"I believe he has directed all his career," del Toro says. "He's a director who has acted for a long time. In many ways, it's the opposite from the way people may perceive him to be."

**LEFT** Cate Blanchett as Lilith. The actress describes *Nightmare Alley* as a cinematic "dark night of the soul—in the darkness, there are three beacons of truth: Molly, Zeena, and Lilith." **RIGHT** Luis Sequeira took inspiration from famous Hollywood sirens when designing some of the luxe gowns Lilith would wear during scenes set at the Copacabana club.

# LILITH RITTER
## CATE BLANCHETT

When Stanton Carlisle meets seductive psychiatrist Lilith Ritter, he has no idea that he's about to be bested at his own game. A member of Buffalo's upper-class elite, Lilith has the connections and status Stan so deeply craves, as well as an innate sophistication born of intellect, education, and old money. Savvy and wise, she senses Stan's greed and his unending need for adoration, and sets out to exploit them, at the same time becoming an object of obsession for the unsuspecting hustler.

What she is not, however, is a traditional femme fatale or a blond with a gun. "It would be very tempting, I think, to play Lilith in that classic noir way," says two-time Academy Award winner Cate Blanchett, who portrays the manipulative character. "But there's more to it than that. Both Guillermo and I wanted her to be someone who was unknowable and mysterious. He kept talking about her being mythical. But at the same time, he was always looking for those little perforations where he could see through to the layers of what would lie underneath—both physically and psychologically."

If anyone could bring layers of depth and nuance to the character, it's Blanchett, who, to great acclaim, has played everyone from Queen Elizabeth in *Elizabeth* (1998) to Bob Dylan in *I'm Not There* (2007). The multi-award-winning actress had been hoping to work with Guillermo del Toro for years, and as much as she relished the role of Lilith, she agreed to star in *Nightmare Alley* principally for the opportunity to collaborate with the filmmaker.

"Guillermo has a powerful and idiosyncratic way of subliminally sneaking contemporary resonances and personal flourishes into the worlds he creates," Blanchett says. "His work has an unsettling quality of seeming strange and far away and familiar, possible and impossible. It's part supernatural, part dark fable, part satire, part noir, part horror—at once unspeakably revolting and deeply beautiful."

For all his films, del Toro writes descriptive biographies for the major characters, detailing their lives up to the point they are introduced in the film. It's a useful tool to help him better understand these people he's created and the forces that have shaped them. As

**ABOVE LEFT** Two of Sequeira's costume sketches depicting Lilith's daytime style for meetings at the office (left) and a chic, full-length dress in burnished gold. **RIGHT** The Lilith's office set included all the hallmarks of art deco. Sequeira even incorporated the bold geometric patterns that are hallmarks of the movement into Lilith's jewelry and accessories.

she began to consider her approach to the role, Blanchett dove into the extensive biography del Toro had created for Lilith—who is described in the script as "an icy woman of indeterminate age and dressed with understated elegance."

From there, Blanchett undertook her own analysis of Lilith's drives and motivations. The actress remained mindful of the work of Swiss psychologist Carl Jung, much in the same way that del Toro had been when developing the character of Stan. "What I did think a lot about in doing this was the Jungian approach to psychology and his sense of archetypes," she says. "He talks a lot about the shadow self, that when one tries to repress the shadow self and to be good and to be kind and to pretend that you don't have these animal drives, the sides that we don't see as civilized, they can erupt in ultimately quite a destructive way."

Echoing Cooper's approach to Stan, Blanchett spent time focusing on how Lilith would speak, crafting a voice that would be hypnotic enough to slowly bend Stan to her will. "With Lilith, I knew that there were these quite long scenes, probably the longest scenes that take place in the film, of a psychoanalytic process gone bad in Lilith's office," Blanchett says. "I knew at some point Stanton would be lying on the couch, and I wanted Lilith's voice to be a voice that could burrow inside his brain, almost like he's in a trance—sort of like a demonic Jiminy Cricket."

Unfortunately for Stan, she's all too successful. "Most people are dying to tell you who they are," del Toro says. "The swindler doesn't escape this rule. He just requires a sharper reader. And Cate Blanchett has that intelligence and that power."

**OPPOSITE** Sitting on the couch in her plush office that she typically reserves for patients, psychiatrist Lilith (Blanchett) strikes a seductive pose during a visit from Stan (Cooper).
**LEFT** The metallic lining of the velvet dress Lilith (Blanchett) wears when she confronts Stan during a nightclub performance was designed to shimmer even in the film's low-light environments.
**ABOVE** Stan's sketch of Lilith.

# MOLLY CAHILL
## ROONEY MARA

Born into carnival life, orphaned Molly has managed to find a sense of family among the troupe of performers, with aging strongman Bruno (Ron Perlman) acting as her surrogate father. She's adored from afar by the Major (Mark Povinelli), Bruno's stage partner, but also loved by all. When Stanton Carlisle enters her life, those closest to Molly are immediately suspicious of his intentions. Molly, too, is wary of the handsome stranger, but ultimately she chooses to set aside her misgivings and allows herself to fall in love with him.

**ABOVE LEFT** Sketches of Molly as seen in Stan's notebook.
**ABOVE RIGHT** Costume sketch by Sequeira of Molly in her signature red dress coat and hat; throughout *Nightmare Alley*, Molly is strongly associated with the color red, symbolizing her deep personal connection to the world of the carnival.
**OPPOSITE** Rooney Mara as Molly, wearing one of the exquisite gowns Stan purchases for her after they move to Buffalo. The costume is made from black velvet and adorned with red and black butterflies.

**ABOVE** A pencil sketch portrait of Molly with the shorter hairstyle she wears while working in the carnival.
**RIGHT** A sketch of Molly in the turn-of-the-century garb she will wear to impersonate the ghost of Ezra Grindle's late lover.
**BELOW** Molly (Rooney Mara) wears a caramel-colored jacket to stay warm when not performing.
**OPPOSITE TOP** Stan (Bradley Cooper) convinces Molly (Mara) to reimagine her carnival act to include an electric chair and the Major (Mark Povinelli) in executioner's garb.

Although Molly is both warm and generous, she's hardly naive, so the character required someone who could simultaneously embody wariness and wisdom as well as a guarded optimism and hopefulness. To play the role, Guillermo del Toro turned to two-time Academy Award–nominated actress Rooney Mara, famed for her performances in 2011's *The Girl with the Dragon Tattoo* and 2015's *Carol*. The filmmaker had been especially taken with her largely silent performance as a grieving widow in David Lowery's meditative 2017 drama *A Ghost Story* and felt that the qualities she brought to that role could also work for Molly.

"Rooney is very almost preternatural," del Toro says. "I thought it would be fantastic to have that nonverbal level with her [as Molly]. The difficult thing about Molly as a character is, she is a carny. At the end of the day, she is not a babe in the woods. Carnies are tough as hell,

so you have this character who has gone through a bunch of things, but she still has a moral compass."

To prepare for the role, Mara watched films from the 1930s and '40s, and, like Blanchett, she spent time focusing on how the character would speak. "We thought maybe she would be Southern, then we decided that was distracting and was a little too similar to Stanton," Mara says. "So we just went with a more subtle way of speaking from that time. I've done a little bit of that before, so it wasn't that new to me. But you want it to feel natural, right? Because in some of those old movies, the actors are putting on a *thing*."

Before filming began, Mara, Cooper, and del Toro spent several days carefully reviewing the script to chart Molly's relationship with Stan and to discuss its intricacies. "I think Stanton's probably pretty similar to her father, who she adored," Mara says. "And he thought she was special, so she was drawn to that. If someone thinks you're special or sees you, you're drawn to them. You think, *Oh, that person gets me*. Obviously, Stan is very charming and came in and swept her off her feet and promised to take care of her. But I think the reality she arrives to is much different than what Stan promised and also what she imagined for herself."

According to the filmmaker, Mara evinced an innate understanding of the character from the start. "I tell you, the way Rooney tracks her characters, she has a wisdom about how much to put in each scene that I think is amazing," del Toro says.

Despite her best efforts, Molly is unable to help Stan rein in his darkest impulses, and she's eventually forced to reconsider the lengths to which she's willing to go to keep this man in her life. "She knows when you're crossing a line," del Toro says. "Stan doesn't."

# ZEENA THE SEER
## TONI COLLETTE

**Played by Oscar-nominated actress Toni Collette, fortune teller Zeena might not truly have the gift of clairvoyance, but she's got a sixth sense about men like Stanton Carlisle. "You're a 'maybe,'" she tells the handsome drifter, "And 'maybes' are real bad for me."**

Intelligent and pragmatic, Zeena wasn't always a small-time carnival performer. After she and her husband, Pete (David Strathairn), then the star of a wildly successful mentalism act, met, the two traveled the world, convincing audiences they were astute clairvoyants. Using a complex system of coded words and phrases, the duo fooled packed crowds into thinking that they could commune with the dead, with Pete relying on Zeena's clues to answer questions from the audience to a shocking degree of specificity.

Eventually, Zeena and Pete came to learn that once people believe they've made contact with loved ones who have passed on, rarely do they find themselves at peace. Instead, they're left craving more interaction, desperately searching for a connection that simply isn't available to them. After offering false hope to so many, Pete found it almost impossible to cope with his guilt, and he succumbed to alcoholism.

With the couple having fallen on hard times, it's Zeena who takes center stage, performing a different take on their classic act. At the carnival, she invites the audience to write questions on slips of paper,

**ABOVE LEFT** A sketch of Zeena, created for Stan's notebook.
**RIGHT** Zeena (Toni Collette) performs in front of an astrology-themed backdrop; her carnival act involves an elaborate ruse in which she "divines" answers to questions from an amazed crowd of onlookers.

which Pete—when he's sober enough—collects in a large basket. Then, a backstage bait-and-switch takes place. A look-alike basket with blank entries is delivered to Zeena, and she sets them on fire to thrill the crowd. Zeena covers her eyes with her hands to channel her powers—but what she's actually doing is looking down through a window in the floor of the stage. There, crouched out of sight, Pete reads through the questions, writing down clues on a chalkboard for Zeena, who then delivers the right answers to the audience.

Rather than lament her lost days of glory, though, Zeena is genuinely content. She loves her husband deeply, despite his crippling addiction, and she considers the other carnival performers to be her family. When Stan comes along, she initiates a sexual relationship with the beguiling newcomer, but her feelings for Stan exist entirely apart from her love for Pete.

"Zeena's relationship with Pete is quite beautiful," Collette says. "They share a lot of history, both good and bad. There is mutual respect, care, and admiration. There is a gentle ease between them and an ever-flowing banter. There is also a certain amount

**ABOVE** Zeena (Toni Collette) relaxes on the porch of the bungalow she rents, located on the periphery of the carnival.
**RIGHT** Zeena (Collette) sits at the table inside her bungalow where she often performs tarot card readings.
**OPPOSITE** As a lucrative side business, Zeena offers personalized horoscopes-by-mail to paying customers. In the early drafts of the *Nightmare Alley* script, Stan reconnects with Zeena some time after his fateful encounter with Grindle in Buffalo and learns that she earns a living creating these astrological charts.

# YOUR PERSONALIZED ASTROLOGICAL
# HOROSCOPE
## by ZEENA
### the ALL SEEING

"I AM CERTAIN THIS FORECAST WILL BE MORE TRUE THAN ANY READING YOU HAVE EVER HAD BEFORE." – ZEENA

Send in the coupon below to get your 2000 word ASTROLOGICAL FORECAST. This reading gives you ASTROLOGICAL Inclinations MONTH by MONTH for the entire year. ZEENA The All Seeing will construct an extensive character delineation based upon an interpretation of your ZODIAC SUN SIGN. It indicates favorable and unfavorable days throughout the year and looks forward to the very beginning of next year. It discusses home life, business affairs, marriage happiness, travel, love and romance, health, friends, vocation, temperament etc. Send only 10¢ coin or stamps and month, day, year and place of birth for this reading.

### Send 10¢ For Your Reading

**25¢ BONUS OFFER!**
'Eye of Providence'
**POWERFUL AMULET**

### To Readers of This Magazine
To all who send their coupon properly completed I will send a personalized ASTROLOGICAL CHART for 10¢. Money MUST be included with the coupon. The CHART will forecast your future as outlined in this advertisement. Please be advised NO REFUNDS.
**Clip and 10¢ SEND NOW!**

**SEND TO: ZEENA** – *The All Seeing,*
**102 GWIN ROAD, ALTOONA, PENNSYLVANIA**

I am enclosing 10¢ for which please send me my personalized ASTROLOGICAL CHART and FREE FORECAST as outlined in your advertisement. I am aware that ZEENA cannot change or control MY FUTURE and reports what she sees in the stars. ZEENA reveals what she sees GOOD or BAD For this reason I understand there is NO REFUND offered.

Birth Date: MONTH.................... DATE............... Year.................

NAME .................................................................................

Address ..............................................................................

City.................................................... State................

that is unsaid. Zeena has real concerns about Pete's waning health, and Pete is concerned about Zeena's wandering eye. There is a kind of unspoken agreement that given their age difference, Zeena is permitted to seek physical pleasure elsewhere. It's just accepted."

Del Toro felt it was important to depict Zeena as someone who "can have an occasional lover and a husband and love each in a different way," he says. "Toni's an incredibly generous and alive actress. I thought she was not only perfect—she was *the* choice."

Collette appreciated that del Toro gave Zeena nuances that humanized the character. Rather than being flighty and eccentric, like a typical movie clairvoyant, Zeena is, in Collette's view, "gutsy and she's real and she's soulful. Really, she's very honest and frank and quite complex in a really unusual way. She's someone who's very comfortable in herself, very aware."

*Nightmare Alley* costume designer Luis Sequeira embraced both aspects of Zeena's personality when creating her wardrobe. The attire she wears onstage at the carnival is more flamboyant and theatrical, though clearly a patched and repaired relic from an earlier era, while her offstage style is quite casual.

"Zeena the Seer had her heyday in the early '20s, when she started doing her original act," Sequeira says. "Her performance dress is an evening dress from the early '20s that has been remodeled. Her robe is a very old, embroidered turquoise velvet robe that she pairs with a gold lamé headscarf. There's a faded glamour to the clothing she wears in this carnival setting. When she's at home, she's very comfortable. She even wears pants. She has a no-nonsense look about her."

Although Stan likes Zeena well enough, he's keenly interested in getting his hands on the code she's developed with Pete to work the crowds. For him, that can't-miss system is a ticket out of the carnival circuit. "She is an intuitive person, but she doesn't get it," Collette says. "He's a master manipulator, and even Zeena, with her innate wisdom, cannot help falling for Stan. He's hot. She's bored. There are fireworks in bed, and she begins to feel things she knows she really shouldn't."

**ABOVE** Concept art of the interior of Zeena's bungalow; Tamara Deverell designed the open space with very low ceilings for dramatic visual effect. "It was just above Bradley Cooper's head height," the production designer says. "He's a tall guy—I don't mind making an actor stoop, but he had to duck into the space. It looked great."
**OPPOSITE TOP RIGHT** Zeena (Toni Collette) performs a tarot card reading for Stan (Cooper).
**OPPOSITE CENTER** Lovers Zeena (Collette) and Stan (Cooper) stand near the shelves in Zeena's bungalow where she displays her collection of knickknacks.
**RIGHT** Concept image depicting the bathroom where Zeena seduces Stan. The room features the same low-slung ceilings as the rest of the bungalow, and an enormous clawfoot tub dominates the space.

# PETE KRUMBEIN
## DAVID STRATHAIRN

**The world of *Nightmare Alley* is beset by sorrow, but few of its characters are as steeped in it as Pete Krumbein. Husband to Zeena, the once wealthy and respectable Pete is now a gentle yet broken man who drinks to excess to silence his conscience. To play the role, del Toro turned to Oscar-nominated actor David Strathairn, known for his work in such films as 2005's *Good Night, and Good Luck* and 2020's *Nomadland*. "David has that air of tragedy combined with dignity and unerring elegance," del Toro says. "He's incredibly smart, and he's a fine, fine instrument. You can tune a performance with David so beautifully."**

Strathairn understood clearly that the guilt Pete carries with him is one of the character's defining traits. "He deceived people and lied to people, which was all part of his act," Strathairn says. "He's had an awakening about what this world is. He's realized that he caused people pain." Still, he becomes an important mentor to Stan—and a cautionary figure as well, warning the young carny against making the same mistakes that blighted his own life.

When Stan comes into their lives, Pete seems to vaguely understand that he and Zeena are having an affair, yet he remains relatively sanguine about it—all he wants in this world is her happiness, and enough booze to dull his senses. "By the time we meet Pete in this film, he realizes that the clock has almost finished ticking for him," Strathairn says. "Not only in the relationship but in the world, in this life. So, he sees Stan and Zeena and says, 'Okay, for her sake, this might be good. I hope this is good.'"

Intrigued as he was by the complexities of the role, Strathairn was also interested in exploring the 1930s carnival world as rendered by del Toro. It's a slice of American history that the actor finds especially fascinating, removed as it is from modern society.

"When I first read the script, I was glad that somebody was making a movie like this about this world," he says. "It's an underbelly of our humanity that is very disturbing, but Guillermo makes it very attractive. The circus has evolved to things like Cirque du Soleil, but this is all about scamming people and deceiving people. There's what you'd call 'lowlifes' everywhere using dead babies in jars and con games and sleight of hand and magic to prey upon our imaginations and our vulnerabilities. This is a palpable world. It has a smell, has a taste. It's far from our daily experience today."

The actor felt further immersed in this world after reading the backstory that del Toro had written for his character, which explored Pete's youth in detail. "It's fun to have gotten inside Guillermo's head as to how he saw this guy," Strathairn says. "It helped. I mean, you can't play your childhood. You can't play your adolescence. You only can play the moment, but it definitely informed me about how he saw Pete. It's like reading a short story about your character. I thought that was a generous thing, and it's a testament to Guillermo's creativity."

For Strathairn, though, the character truly sprang to life once he was on set in the carnival environment, working with Bradley Cooper and Toni Collette to form the relationships that seal Pete's fate. "Toni's electric," Strathairn says. "She's alive, as Zeena needs to be—that's what I think Pete saw [in her]. Bradley, he's so present, listens really well, as Stan needs to. Stan's focused on what he needs to glean from Pete, and Pete sees that. He sees himself in Stan."

**OPPOSITE LEFT** A sketch of Pete from Stan's notebook.
**OPPOSITE RIGHT** Husband and wife team Pete (David Strathairn) and Zeena (Toni Collette).
**TOP** Pete (Strathairn) demonstrates some classic showmanship techniques.
**ABOVE** Pete (Strathairn) and Stan (Bradley Cooper) develop an unlikely father-son rapport.

**OPPOSITE** Willem Dafoe as Clem, the mustachioed carnival barker who serves as a patriarchal figure for the troupe.
**LEFT** Clem takes a break from his carnival duties to smoke a cigarette.
**ABOVE** A sketch of Clem from Stan's notebook.

# CLEM HOATELY
## WILLEM DAFOE

Mustachioed carnival barker Clem Hoately serves as Stanton Carlisle's entrée into the underworld. After Stan spies Molly at a bus stop café, he follows her to the bright lights of the carnival tent where showman Clem is luring the locals to come take a gander at a creature who appears to be neither man nor beast—the geek. Like a man hypnotized, Stan follows Clem's summons and gets an eyeful of the terrible show.

"My character's the guy that runs this ten-in-one, which is basically the sideshow," says actor Willem Dafoe, who plays Clem. "He's a barker, of course, out there . . . enticing people to come in, [and he] has a bit of con in him. He wants to get people what they need so he can make a dollar. When Stan comes in, he recognizes there's something not right about this guy. This guy is a little off. He's a little sleazy. He's on the make. He recognizes himself in Stan."

A four-time Oscar nominee known for his ability to slip into the skin of a wide range of characters, Dafoe had long been interested in working with Guillermo del Toro, having been a fan of his filmography. They became better acquainted following the release of Julian Schnabel's 2018 biographical drama *At Eternity's Gate*, in which the actor played Vincent van Gogh in the last years of his life. Del Toro was a vocal supporter of the film.

"He spoke very beautifully about that film, better than Julian and I did, and that was quite impressive," Dafoe says. "We were in touch. He simply said, 'Listen, I have this film I'm doing, and I have something for you to do in it.' In early talks, he was vague about which role, then finally he zeroed in on Clem Hoately, and that was it really. He sent me the script, and I was eager to work with him. I thought it was a role that was interesting to do. It wasn't a complicated negotiation."

With his two-tone heeled boots and his faded crimson-and-

**CLOCKWISE FROM TOP LEFT** Clem's wife, Louise (Lara Jean Chorostecki), as the carnival's Spider Woman (her act was based on one that del Toro saw as a child in Mexico); Clem (Willem Dafoe) explains to a curious Stan (Bradley Cooper) how exactly one convinces a man to "geek"; Clem (Dafoe) brings Stan (Cooper) into the carnival fold; Clem (Dafoe) holds one of the bottles of alcohol he sells to his performers—he maintains two stashes, one of consumable booze and another of wood alcohol.

gold barker's jacket, Clem is certainly one of the carnival's more colorful characters. Whether he's in wily showman mode or acting as cutthroat circus impresario, his demeanor is always intimidating and unpredictable. He's the carnival's patriarch, caring and tender toward his pregnant wife, Louise (Lara Jean Chorostecki), who performs as the Spider-Woman, yet unfathomably cruel to the addicts he lures into the carnival to work as geeks.

"He's a heavy guy," Dafoe says. "He does some things that aren't so nice, but it's also clear that there's some goodness in him—you see that in glimpses with how he treats his wife. You see it with the kind of skewed code that he has. It's kind of a carny code. His whole point of view is an us-and-them mentality . . . I always like characters where what you see is not what you get."

Growing up in Wisconsin in the late '50s and early '60s, Dafoe recalls occasionally encountering hardscrabble men like Clem. "Carnivals like this with freak shows and geek shows don't exist anymore, but I remember, as a child, they still existed to some degree," he says. "I remember those guys, they were scary. They were smoothies, you know. They'd try to be sweet, but you could see, underneath, they had a kind of get-over-on-you criminality. They were guys that would size you up and say, 'What can I get from this person?' rather than 'What can I give to this person?' This is from another era, but it's very much made out of a very specific American character."

Although he mined his own past when developing the character, Dafoe says he really hooked into the language of the era, captured so beautifully in del

Toro and Kim Morgan's screenplay. "It's fun to work with language that's elevated," Dafoe says. "It carries with it all the flavor and atmosphere of a time and an attitude and a way of being. You don't just say, 'I'm going out the door.' It's much more colorful to say—I'm making this up—'I'm out skidoo.' Even if you don't know what that means, it has a life to it. It has an energy. Some of the expressions, you're not even quite sure what they mean, but they have a flavor that's so juicy that you get character, tone, and even in some cases psychology from them."

He also derived ideas about Clem from the details of the costume Luis Sequeira had designed for the character. "It was clear that there was a slight vanity to him," Dafoe says. "He was probably better looking and had more strut once upon a time. Now, he's getting a little older, he's been around, but he still maintains a pride in certain things. He can be living in the middle of a tent, in the middle of animal dung, but he still keeps these shoes looking good. He's got a nice leather jacket. He's a guy that really believes that what you present tells a lot about you. After all, he's a barker, so he's very much about convincing people, influencing people, and also suckering people."

Says del Toro of Dafoe: "You believe he's in a carnival in the '30s and '40s. You believe that he's married to the Spider-Woman. Willem is, in my opinion, the embodiment of the carnival."

**OPPOSITE LEFT** Luis Sequeira's design for Clem's costume included a blazer and vest, along with stylish two-tone boots.
**ABOVE** Concept art depicting the Salvation Army shelter where Clem and Stan leave the carnival's ailing geek once he becomes too ill to perform.
**LEFT** Clem (Dafoe) and Stan (Cooper) stand over the unconscious body of the geek (Paul Anderson) after a violent tussle inside the carnival's fun house.

**OPPOSITE** Bruno (Ron Perlman) performs feats of strength for carnival attendees.
**FAR LEFT** Bruno (Perlman) clad in the fur-trimmed jacket that he often wears onstage and off.
**LEFT** Bruno sketches from Stan's notebook.

# BRUNO THE STRONGMAN
## RON PERLMAN

After Ron Perlman watched 1947's *Nightmare Alley* for the first time, he remembers being haunted by it. "I already was a big fan of Tyrone Power from *The Mark of Zorro* and a number of the other films that he'd done, [playing] kind of straight-ahead, very handsome leading men, very affable characters," Perlman says. "And here he is in this thing, which is so shady and so dark, playing a character of real questionable morality. I was fascinated with his choice to be in it. My estimation of him as an artist just went through the roof."

Still, he always felt that more could have been done with the material. "There was a lot of room for a bigger film," Perlman says. "The journey of Stan Carlisle is almost biblical, certainly Shakespearean, very operatic, very Greek theater. A guy who's been blessed with this incredible skill set and hubris ends up taking him out."

When Perlman and the filmmaker watched *Nightmare Alley* together after their fateful conversation on the *Cronos* set, del Toro became just as taken with the movie as his friend had been. "It got under his skin," Perlman recalls. "It was almost revelatory to see him discover it for the first time. His eyes were the size of flying saucers."

Decades later, with del Toro finally on the cusp of making his own version of Gresham's novel, the filmmaker naturally wanted to create a role for Perlman that would play to his many talents. Bruno, the carnival's aging strongman, proved to be ideal. "Ron is so carny," del Toro says. "Ron could say lines that are period lines, and he has the voice and the import to say them. Just by standing in the frame, he's incredibly interesting as an actor."

Acting as a kind of elder statesman for the carnival, Bruno is part of a weightlifting and wrestling act opposite his longtime stage partner, "Major Mosquito" (Mark Povinelli), who is billed as "the smallest human on Earth."

Visually, the pair stands in stark contrast to one another, but from a personality standpoint, they are surprisingly alike. "You've got this big, hulky, seventy-year-old dude with this little person who's an Edward G. Robinson kinda guy," Perlman says. "To watch them in performance mode, and then to watch them just walking around and see why they spend so much time together, how philosophically similar they are, is a cool aspect of the movie. They're two sides of the same coin. They have the same values. They have the same respect for the carnival world. They have the same instincts."

They also have the same loving attitude toward Molly, though Bruno is very much a father figure to Rooney Mara's character, while the Major is lovestruck. "Her old man and I were best friends," says Perlman. "When he passed away, he asked me to keep my eye on her, so I become her constant surrogate dad. I'm very protective of her. So, when Stan comes around, that makes for a real kind of friction [and] tension. He's like the rooster that walks into the coop and wants to take over. Everything we [think] about him turns out to be true."

# THE MAJOR
## MARK POVINELLI

**If there's anyone less impressed by Stanton Carlisle than Bruno, it's his counterpart, the Major, a surly carnival veteran who—rightly—worries that the drifter's arrival will eventually lead to tragedy.**

To play the Major, del Toro needed an actor who would not only have great give-and-take chemistry with Ron Perlman but also express the character's unrequited crush on Molly with true tenderness. "I didn't want to have the forlorn secret lover be sappy," says the writer-director. "I wanted a guy that was tough, that knew his way around the world and wasn't fooled by Stan and could be protective [toward Molly] without being sappy."

Del Toro found his man in veteran stage and screen actor Mark Povinelli, whose credits include *Water for Elephants* (2011), *Mirror Mirror* (2012), and *My Dinner with Hervé* (2018). "The camera loves to look at him," del Toro says. "He is incredibly expressive with few lines and brings that power and dignity and strength to the character."

Povinelli says he was drawn to *Nightmare Alley* in part because of the respect with which it treats the carnival performers. "I've spent a lot of time fascinated by the early twentieth century carnivals—the way people like myself and other people who are obviously different existed back then and also used the system to their advantage," says the three-foot-nine-inch actor. "Guillermo has dedicated a fair amount of time in this movie to these characters that make up the fabric of the carnival. Usually in these films, if they're set in a carnival or some kind of circus, they're there as visual aids."

On set, Povinelli and Perlman quickly developed a rapport between their characters that Povinelli describes as not unlike that of "an old married couple." He adds: "We've been together for a long time. We work together. We sleep in the same trucks. We have to get along. But it's constant bickering. But we're always by each other's side and know what the other one's thinking without even saying it."

**OPPOSITE** The Major (Mark Povinelli) pummels Bruno (Ron Perlman) as part of the duo's wrestling act.
**ABOVE** The Major (Povinelli) is among the carnival performers who pay a visit to Stan and Molly at their Buffalo hotel room.
**BOTTOM LEFT** A sketch of The Major for Stan's notebook.
**BOTTOM RIGHT** A Guy Davis concept for The Major in executioner's garb.

# EZRA GRINDLE
## RICHARD JENKINS

**Richard Jenkins last worked with Guillermo del Toro on** *The Shape of Water*, **playing the sweet-natured Giles, a closeted gay man in his late sixties who comes to the aid of the film's heroine and her amphibian soulmate. It was a performance that earned Jenkins his second Oscar nomination—his first came for his performance as a widowed college professor in Tom McCarthy's 2007 drama** *The Visitor*. **In** *Nightmare Alley*, **however, Jenkins steps into a role that is worlds away from the gentle character he inhabited in del Toro's earlier film.**

Ezra Grindle is the most influential man in Buffalo, an imposing magnate who has amassed untold wealth. Despite his riches, he's blind to all that he possesses. He fixates instead on a great wrong from his past, blaming himself for causing the death of a woman he loved. After Stan arrives in the city and learns Grindle's secrets with the help of Lilith Ritter, he comes to believe he can exploit the older man's all-consuming grief to further his own fortunes.

"I really loved this character," Jenkins says. "I loved the idea of him. He's got more money than anybody, and I don't think it means anything to him. He's just totally obsessed with this young girl that he did wrong by. I loved the idea of somebody spending his whole life thinking about [this woman] and what he did [to hurt her]. This love of his has been magnified in his brain. He's just obsessed and filled with guilt."

Not only was Jenkins eager to play Grindle, but he also felt a strong personal connection to the world in which the film takes place. When he was growing up in DeKalb, Illinois, his father took him to a small-town carnival that included a geek show. "Guillermo has never seen one!" says the seventy-four-year-old actor. "Nobody else [on the film] had ever seen one. But I'm the old guy there, so I happened to see the last of this stuff that became illegal—and rightfully so. It should be illegal. It was this guy, and they threw a dead chicken into a cage with him, and he started tearing at it with his teeth and growling. It was horrifying."

Grindle's imposing office and his palatial estate in Buffalo couldn't be more different from the shabby carnival world. His environments are stately and stolid, built from only the finest materials and decorated with the most expensive furnishings. "[His office is] a place [where] when you come in, you're intimidated because it's so opulent," Jenkins says. Similarly, the gardens that surround his home are immaculate, serving as a tribute to the memory of the woman whose forgiveness appears to lie beyond his grasp. "It's a thirst he can't quench," Jenkins says.

His wardrobe, too, was tailored to suit a man holding a vast fortune; to further look the part, Jenkins grew a beard and wore a hairpiece and eyeglasses. "Guillermo wanted [the clothes] to say 'money,'" Jenkins says. "They were beautiful, but they were so heavy that I could barely stand up in them sometimes. I had an overcoat that must have been thirty pounds ... You were warm in this thing."

**THESE PAGES** One of the wealthiest men in Buffalo, Ezra Grindle (Richard Jenkins) becomes the target of Stan's schemes. Jenkins was previously nominated for an Oscar for his supporting performance in Guillermo del Toro's *The Shape of Water*.

**THESE PAGES** Holt McCallany cuts an intimidating figure as Anderson, Grindle's no-nonsense bodyguard. When del Toro contacted McCallany to offer him the role, the actor was aboard a train in France. Recalls McCallany, "The voice on the other end of the phone says, 'Holt! It's Guillermo del Toro! I have a film with Bradley Cooper. It would be an honor for me if you would come to be in my film.' I was so stunned that I can't even describe the feeling."

# ANDERSON
## HOLT MCCALLANY

**Despite his outward confidence, Stanton Carlisle inspires nothing but skepticism and distrust among the select few perceptive enough to read him the way he can read others. Ezra Grindle's bodyguard, known simply as Anderson, is one of those people. A former soldier who's head of the millionaire's security detail, the character is played by Holt McCallany, known for his role as FBI agent Bill Tench in David Fincher's acclaimed drama *Mindhunter*, which focuses on the founding of the agency's Behavioral Science Unit.**

"Guillermo felt that Anderson needed to be an intimidating presence because he's really the one—more than anyone else—who sees through Stanton," McCallany says. "From the beginning, Anderson is the guy who says, 'No, I don't buy it.' He's a guy with a deeply suspicious nature, and he seizes upon little things about Stanton that he doesn't like—and he's proven right in the end."

Del Toro offered the role to McCallany after seeing his work on *Mindhunter*, feeling that he had the requisite stoic menace. Although Anderson's dialogue in the *Nightmare Alley* script is sparse, McCallany says he jumped at the opportunity to work with del Toro, and was excited by the creative challenge the part presented.

"Sometimes performers in film don't understand the power of motionlessness, stillness," McCallany says. "Sometimes a character who is very smart—because Anderson's no dummy—and is really listening and watching and processing what he's seeing, he can be a big presence in a scene. But it takes a great director to stage that in a way that really tells that story, and that's what Guillermo was able to do with my character. Often, you simply see me watching, lurking, listening, thinking. We're never quite sure what Anderson is thinking—but we understand that what he does not have is trust in Stanton Carlisle."

## CHAPTER THREE
# THE WORLD

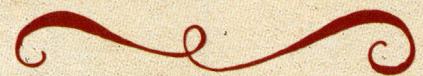

*Within a circling garland a girl dances; the beasts of the Apocalypse look on.*

As it charts the rise and fall of Cooper's aspiring con man, *Nightmare Alley* brings to life two distinct worlds: the traveling carnival, long since past its prime, and the more glamorous city of Buffalo, where Stanton comes to ply his craft for the amusement of wealthy clientele.

To develop the evocative visual language for each half of the film, del Toro relied on collaborators including cinematographer Dan Laustsen, costume designer Luis Sequeira, and production designer Tamara Deverell, who also had worked on *Mimic* and del Toro's apocalyptic vampire series *The Strain*, which ran on the FX Network from 2014 to 2017. Visual effects supervisor Dennis Berardi, founder of Toronto-based VFX house Mr. X, completed the team.

Lighting, color, costume, and makeup effects are integral to any del Toro production, and through the decades, the filmmaker has developed a singular aesthetic that is truly unmistakable. Although *Nightmare Alley* features many of his usual hallmarks, it also sees him branching into new creative territory.

The film's composition and color palette were largely inspired by visual artists from the early twentieth century. Dane Vilhelm Hammershøi, famed for his meditative portraits of interiors and other architectural spaces rendered in muted hues, was an influence. So, too, were American realist painters such as George Bellows, Edward Hopper, and Andrew Wyeth, all of whom depicted stolen moments in the lives of everyday people from the early decades of the 1900s.

"I loved the idea of making an America that was closer to those guys," del Toro says. "I think they have a harshness, the way they light, the way they compose their color palette. I wanted to use those olive greens and the reds and those shapes. Those guys existed at a time

when America goes from the dream of the pastoral to a harsher urban reality, particularly Hopper. He embodies that transition."

From the start, del Toro, Deverell, and the others planned to make each half of Stanton's story feel like a discrete environment with its own signature palette and design elements. The art deco movement would rule the latter half of the film, but for the carnival, Deverell took inspiration from the vivid colors embraced by artists belonging to the fauvist school, such as Henri Matisse.

"There was a color palette that was very bright and intense, and it was almost as if we very intentionally took a yellow wash and put it over the whole thing," the production designer says. "Dan Laustsen's lighting helped tone it down, so it [didn't look like] a kid's movie or anything like that. When Stan Carlisle moves into Buffalo, that became more about patterns and geometry and finishes like bronzes and polished wood and art deco colors that are more muted and sophisticated and subtle. I didn't try to blend them together. I was embracing their differences as much as I could."

Laustsen opted to use the Alexa 65mm digital camera, which boasts an impressive depth of field—meaning it could capture *Nightmare Alley*'s detailed sets and locations as well as the nuances of the actors' performances. Additionally, it was ideal for many of the very low-light environments where Stan finds himself as the narrative

**ABOVE** Concept art depicting Stan's arrival at the bus stop café where he first spies Molly, Bruno, and The Major. The look of *Nightmare Alley* was strongly inspired by American realist painters such as Edward Hopper, perhaps best known for his 1942 oil painting *Nighthawks*.
**OPPOSITE BOTTOM LEFT** Bradley Cooper and Rooney Mara between scenes on the bus stop café set.
**OPPOSITE BOTTOM RIGHT** Guillermo del Toro confers with his leading man on the café set.

**ABOVE** Concept art of the bus stop café interior.
**OPPOSITE TOP** Makeup artists offer touch-ups to Mark Povinelli (seated) and Ron Perlman during shooting of the bus stop café scenes.
**OPPOSITE BOTTOM** An additional bus stop café concept shows the establishment filled with diners.

unfolds. "Guillermo really was pushing me into the darkness," Laustsen says. "I'm a pretty dark cinematographer. I really like to make it dark, but on this show, in some scenes, it's *really* dark. But it did ultimately work well."

Although *Nightmare Alley* might be dark—both visually and thematically—del Toro was adamant that the film should not contain any stereotypically noir trappings: "We didn't want any of the clichés like venetian blinds and fans and smoky atmospheres," he says. "We wanted to evoke classical lighting."

Both del Toro and Laustsen sought to make a period film that was rooted in the 1930s and '40s but at the same time felt contemporary. "We are much more colorful than you would be normally [in a film from that era]," says the Danish cinematographer. "A movie in the '40s would be desaturated with not so much color, maybe more brown, but we're not there. We use color a lot to tell the story, and that's coming from Guillermo. We really try to play with the light, play with the camera movement."

In terms of direction, del Toro deviated from the approach he'd employed on his previous sets. After a successful take, normally he would reposition the camera so that he could film the scene again, this time with one of the actors in close-up. On *Nightmare Alley*, del Toro instead composed a

"moving master" shot that kept the key players in frame, allowing every take to fully play out, with the aim of giving the actors time to lose themselves in their performance without interruption.

"I started to do many, many masters that crossed each other, allowing the actors to run the scene from beginning to end, which I've never really done," del Toro says. "Bradley and Rooney, Cate, Willem—I needed to give them the space to play the whole scene. It came about also because I had studied classical filmmaking. I wanted to be unobtrusive with the camera. I didn't want to do flashy camera moves. I wanted to do these two-, three-, four-minute masters that just flowed."

# A NIGHTMARE SCENARIO

After months of preproduction during which casting was finalized and the creative team completed their planning and design work, *Nightmare Alley* began filming on January 16, 2020. While the interior scenes set in 1941 Buffalo would be filmed at the beginning of the planned seventy-six-day shoot, many of the carnival sequences were scheduled to be shot on location during late spring. Filming began at one of Toronto's newest production facilities, a sprawling studio location known as the Netflix hub, with *Nightmare Alley* taking over two of the facility's four soundstages.

Eight weeks after cameras had begun to roll, things changed dramatically when the COVID-19 pandemic forced the world into lockdown. The filmmakers had been keeping an eye on the troubling rise in case numbers around the world throughout February and into early March, and as the days passed, it quickly became clear that it would be impossible to continue filming without endangering the health and safety of the cast and crew. So, on March 12, 2020, during the production's lunch break, the decision was made to shut down.

"The way COVID started, we thought it was going to be contained," del Toro says. "The more it kept spreading, the more we felt we needed to stop. It was not mandatory nor expected, but we were very supported by Searchlight. [I worried that] somebody [was] going to be sick, and I didn't want to have that responsibility. It would be terrible. So we stopped."

At that point, the filmmaker assumed the break would last no more than ten weeks. Like millions the world over, he remained indoors in quarantine, waiting to see how the situation evolved. Unfortunately, "it kept evolving for the worst," del Toro says.

Realizing that the cast and crew would be unable to return to filming

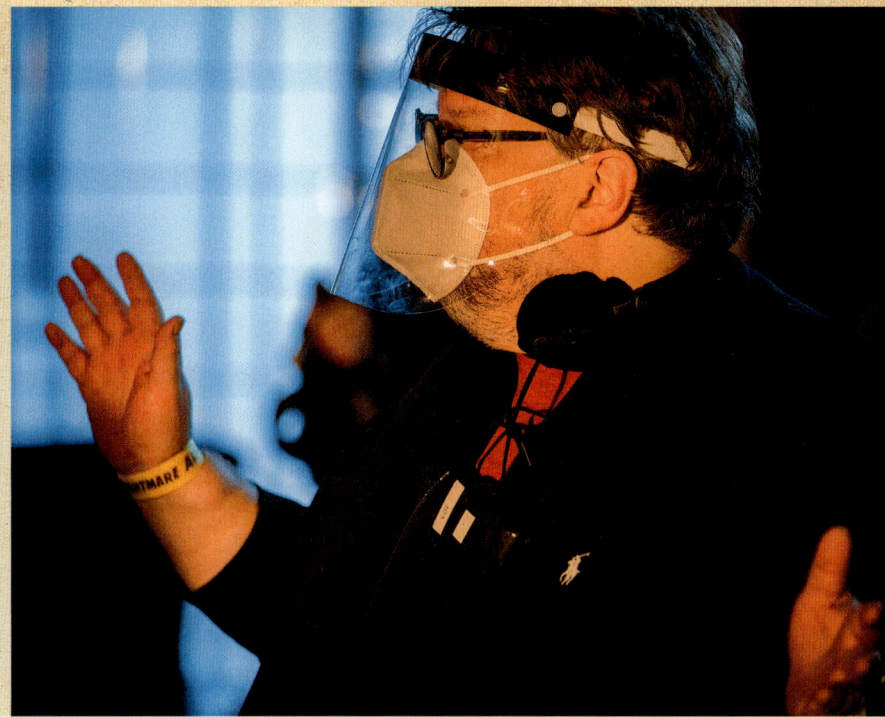

anytime soon, producer J. Miles Dale arranged for the standing sets to remain undisturbed on the production's soundstages. He also worked with the department heads to ensure that all the props, costumes, and other necessary items for the shoot were placed in safekeeping. Then he set out to learn everything he could about the deadly illness.

"Once the housekeeping was done, I can't tell you how many hours a week I spent educating myself about the virus, what the testing options were, waiting for the unions to come up with [protocols]," Dale says. "The things that you need to know to be a producer, none of that really matters anymore. You find yourself being on the phone with lab technicians."

With the border between the United States and Canada closed, del Toro remained in Toronto, where he began to edit the footage that had been shot before the shutdown. Working remotely, he and Cooper had the rare opportunity to spend time poring over the sequences together and discussing the best way to approach the remaining scenes. Through it all, del Toro says his star never wavered in his commitment to the film. "There was an immersion and a fusion between the two of us that without the pandemic wouldn't have happened," del Toro says.

After six months, *Nightmare Alley* resumed production in Toronto on September 16, 2020, with strict COVID-19 mitigation strategies in place, including masking, distancing, and rigorous testing (Dale says the production conducted upward of 17,000 COVID tests). "When we came back, it was like shooting in a surgical theater," del Toro says. "We were shooting with masks and shields and gloves. Every few minutes you had to sanitize your hands. We had a lot of limitations, and all of it got in the way, but at the end of the day, you got what you needed, same as always."

Adds Dale: "Starting up again, there were land mines everywhere, but you had to find a way to keep a happy set—a creative, anxiety-free set—but still have these rules. The restart was very different from the first pass. We lost a lot of days. [The original schedule was for a total of] seventy-six days, and [because of COVID], we ended up at ninety-two, not something that a producer would normally advertise. But stuff just took longer, and you couldn't rush it."

Postproduction would later also be severely affected: score recordings, mixing rooms, and some editorial needed to be carried out remotely or in isolated sessions, resulting in a much-elongated process. "What normally would take a few weeks took months," del Toro says. "We kept having to do face testing, schedule vaccinations, and keep a minimum amount of people in working sessions."

**OPPOSITE** The COVID-19 pandemic forced *Nightmare Alley* into an unexpected months-long hiatus. When filming resumed, everyone on set—including Ron Perlman and Mark Povinelli, seen here waiting to film a scene in character as Bruno and The Major—adhered to strict safety protocols such as masking and social distancing.
**ABOVE LEFT** Star Bradley Cooper, pictured here between scenes as Stan, wearing a surgical mask.
**ABOVE RIGHT** Guillermo del Toro directs from behind a face shield.

## BURNING DOWN THE HOUSE

Stanton Carlisle's descent into hell begins in a room enveloped in flame. Inside the remote country shack where he spent his childhood, Stan drags a heavy object across the wooden floor into what appears to be a freshly dug grave. Tipping over several canisters of gasoline, he lights a match, and soon the rotting boards of the dilapidated structure are consumed in the conflagration. He walks into the twilight toward his new life without pausing to glance at the destruction he's left behind him. The unsettling sequence serves as the ominous prelude to *Nightmare Alley*, establishing Stan's sociopathic character and foreshadowing his eventual self-destruction.

Although William Lindsay Gresham's novel opens with Stan already embedded in the world of the carnival, del Toro felt it was important to peer briefly into Stan's background and to present the audience with a central mystery concerning the forces that shaped him early on. "I needed a big question mark," del Toro says. "I thought it would be really interesting to do this [opening sequence] where you see a thing he's trying to escape—[his past]. There's a person that weighs heavily on him. He thinks he can get rid of him, and he can't."

Only much later does del Toro reveal the truth of what happened—Stan was hauling his father's body into the unmarked grave. All that is left behind by the dead man is his watch, an inexpensive timepiece made of brass that he nevertheless prized dearly. It's one of the few possessions Stan has when *Nightmare Alley* begins, and he continues

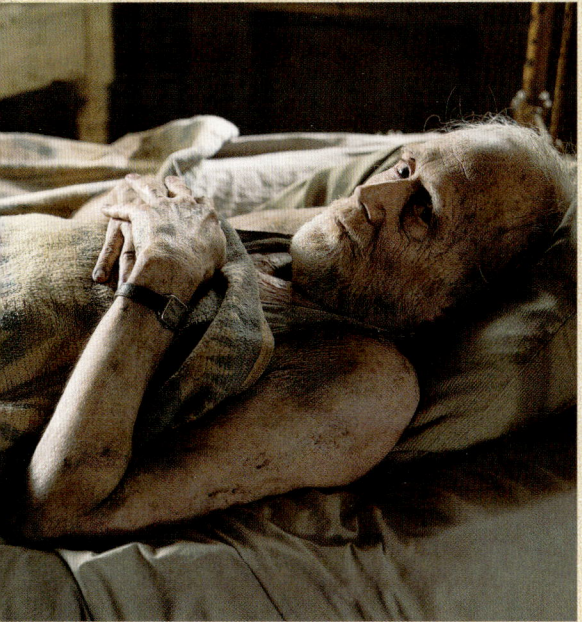

**OPPOSITE** Concept art depicts the interior of the modest cabin where Stan grew up.
**ABOVE** Concept art of the cabin in flames after Stan sets the structure alight.
**FAR LEFT** Stan's ailing father (William McDonald) clings to life, his prized watch on his wrist.
**LEFT** Stan (Bradley Cooper) contemplates a terrible sin.

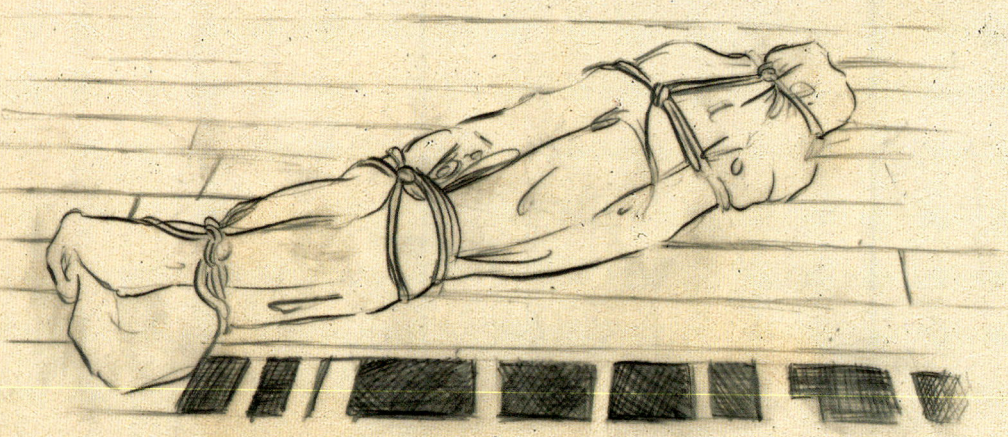

to wear it even after he has the means to purchase something far grander; it becomes a kind of talisman for the character.

The interior of the two-room shack was modeled on a similarly modest home on display at Canada's Black Creek Pioneer Village, an open-air Ontario museum set up to illustrate what life was like in the region from the 1790s to the 1860s. "What we built was this disheveled, falling-apart, rotting boards, rotting cracked windows, ceiling caving in kind of space," Deverell says.

Onscreen, Stan ignites the blaze, but on set, it was the special effects team that managed the controlled burn. Later, in postproduction, visual effects supervisor Berardi embellished the flames to make the sequence more harrowing. Much like the complexities of computer-generated hair or fur, "digital fire is very hard to get right," he says.

"Fire is this natural phenomenon that has this kind of volumetric chaos, this flicker ratio, this contrast ratio, the intensity and speed, little embers coming off," Berardi continues. "If you don't get all that chaos right, it looks flat. We developed a

volumetric fire system that is not flat or 2D . . . I don't think anyone can tell the difference in this movie [as to] which is the digital fire and which is the practical fire. They play alongside each other a lot."

For the exterior scenes of Stan walking away from the shack, del Toro wanted to replicate the eerie stillness of Andrew Wyeth's 1948 painting *Christina's World*, which depicts a young woman lying in a field staring at a farmhouse in the distance. The production team built the exterior of Stan's dilapidated childhood home on location in Tottenham, Ontario, about an hour outside of Toronto, striving to re-create Wyeth's haunting tableau.

"We looked everywhere for this perfect hill—we were scouting and scouting," Deverell says. "Dan Laustsen and I found it in sync with each other. We positioned the shack so that we'd be able to get this incredible shot with the sun setting behind it." The idea was that the light from the setting sun would bathe the scene in the same muted gold, green, and brown tones that Wyeth had used for his classic landscape painting. "Unfortunately, when we went to burn it down, the sun wasn't where we wanted it to be," Deverell says.

To compensate for the inclement weather, del Toro relied on digital effects, tweaking the color of the ominous early evening sky and the arrangements of the clouds in postproduction. But like many of the eight hundred visual effects shots in *Nightmare Alley*, the computer-generated adjustments were designed to blend seamlessly into the real-world photography. "Anytime Guillermo wanted to have these foreboding skies, these *Wuthering Heights*–type skies, we did that digitally," Berardi says. "Most of the skies are replaced in the movie. We added lightning and really profound, moody clouds."

Adds del Toro: "If you're trying to [pay homage] to Grant Wood or Hopper or any of these painters that we used as reference, you need a certain type of sky that is very much part of the language of Americana. We created some amazing skies that give a level of painterly stylization to the movie. We also lucked out and had some skies where you think, 'Oh, that must be digital,' but they're real."

**OPPOSITE TOP LEFT** Stan (Cooper) drags a corpse toward a freshly dug grave.
**OPPOSITE CENTER** Concept art showing how the body would be positioned beneath the cabin's wooden floor boards.
**OPPOSITE BOTTOM** A sketch from Stan's notebook of a corpse wrapped in canvas and tied with rope.
**ABOVE** On location, Bradley Cooper films the scene in which Stan walks away from the burning cabin.

# WELCOME TO THE CARNIVAL

**From the ashes of his childhood home, Stan hopes to rise a new man, but for a poor, hungry drifter, affluence can be hard to come by.** "I think of Pinocchio or Frankenstein's monster in a strange way," del Toro says when discussing Stan. "These are essentially lonely characters, all of them. Stan is as lonely as them. Look at the way he starts [the film]. He's wandering with a radio in a little bag, and that's all he has. He could have landed in an oil field or an orchestra, but he landed in a carnival."

During the 1920s and '30s, it wasn't uncommon to find men like Stan earning a living as carnival hands. After the 1893 Chicago World's Fair, which generated interest around the country, carnivals became wildly popular in regions outside America's bigger cities. People who lived in the small towns and rural outposts of the late nineteenth and early twentieth centuries tended to have less disposable income and fewer entertainment options, so the arrival of a traveling carnival with its bright lights and thrilling rides became a noteworthy event.

As time went on, however, the carnival also earned a reputation as a haven for the seedier elements of society—misfits or felons who made their living by scamming unsuspecting patrons. "What is compelling for me about that reality is that the carnival is an incredibly close society," del Toro says. "Since its origins, the

**LEFT** In this concept image of the carnival at night, the entrance gates are illuminated by strings of bulbs emitting a warm, entrancing glow.
**BELOW** Built to scale on location at Canada's Markham Fairgrounds, *Nightmare Alley*'s sprawling carnival incarnations (one movie, two carnivals) were truly impressive pieces of production design, featuring a labyrinthine fun house and a functioning merry-go-round and Ferris wheel. The neon sign pillars were del Toro's visual quotation to Hitchcock's *Strangers on a Train* carnival entrance.

carnival has been almost as close to a sect as possible. People don't reveal the secrets. People are very guarded. Most of the people in the carnival have escaped a life of crime and have a past to leave behind, yet they form a strong solidarity. They are incredibly close to each other. They protect each other."

Creating *Nightmare Alley*'s carnival was an enormous undertaking. Rather than building a series of sets on a soundstage, del Toro always planned to construct a real carnival on location. "The difference between building those tents in the comfort of a stage or the real place means that a piece of fabric flies, straw gets disturbed by the wind," he says. "The wind blows through the tents and makes them breathe. It's amazing."

Working from hundreds of reference images from the late 1920s and the 1930s, Deverell began designing the physical layout for the

*(Continued on page 83)*

**OPPOSITE TOP** A concept illustration of the Spider Woman's stage by Guy Davis.
**OPPOSITE BOTTOM** Concept image of the carnival's backstage areas, where many of the performers live.
**ABOVE** Molly (Rooney Mara) and Stan (Bradley Cooper) flirt tentatively at the carnival's carousel.
**LEFT** Sketches of the carousel horses created for Stan's notebook.

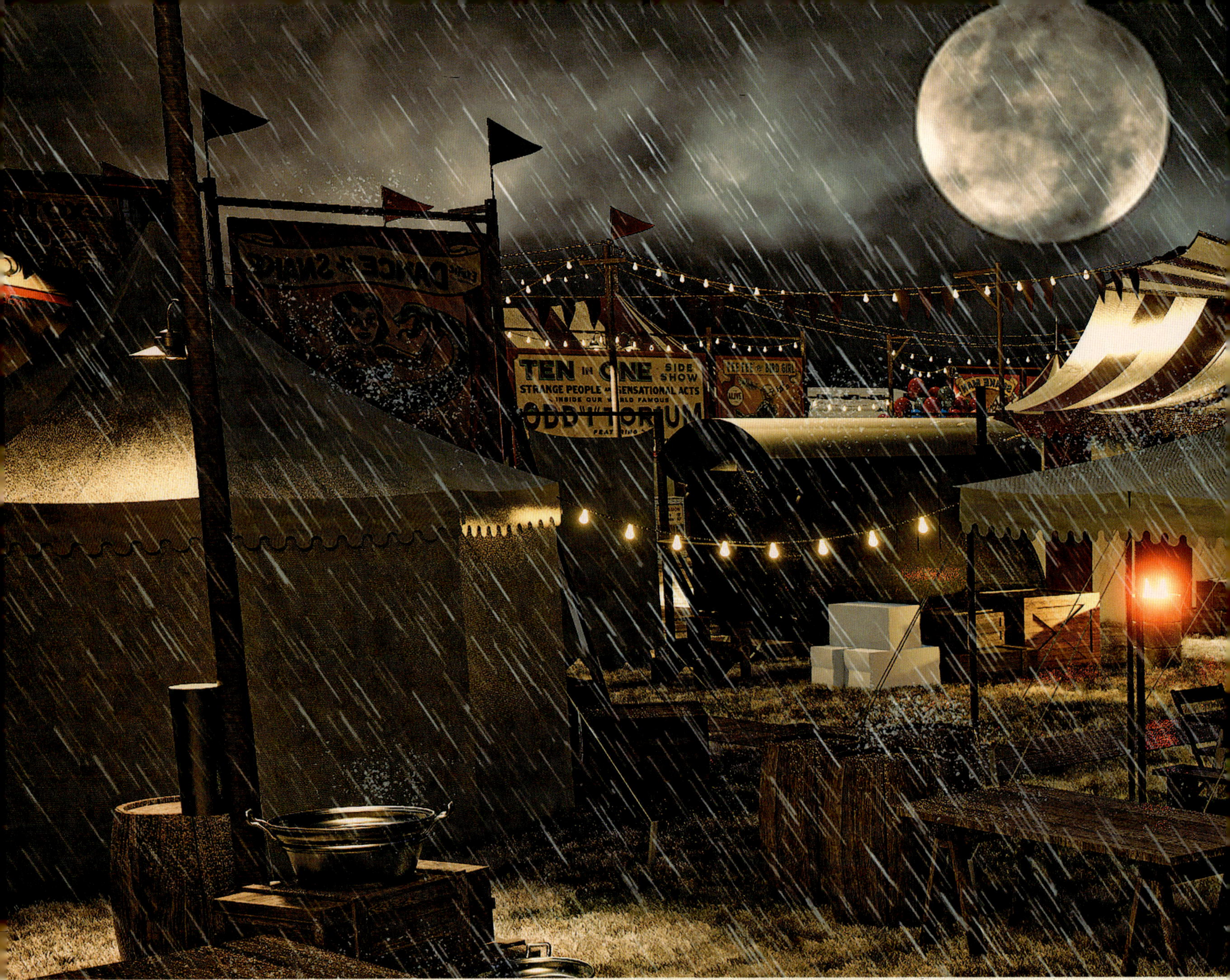
TEN IN ONE SIDE SHOW
STRANGE PEOPLE SENSATIONAL ACTS
INSIDE OUR WORLD FAMOUS
ALIVE

MYSTIC ZEENA SEERESS
SHE KNOWS ALL
MENTALIST
ZEENA
TELLS ALL for 50¢
the PSYCHIC
FANTASTIC
She GIVES ADVICE ON
LOVE AFFAIRS
BUSINESS MATTERS
DIVORCE CASES

DANCE OF THE SNAKE
ALIVE
EXOTIC and UNUSUAL
STEP INSIDE
Sultan's Pleasure Dome
WITNESS THE DANCE OF THE SNAKE!

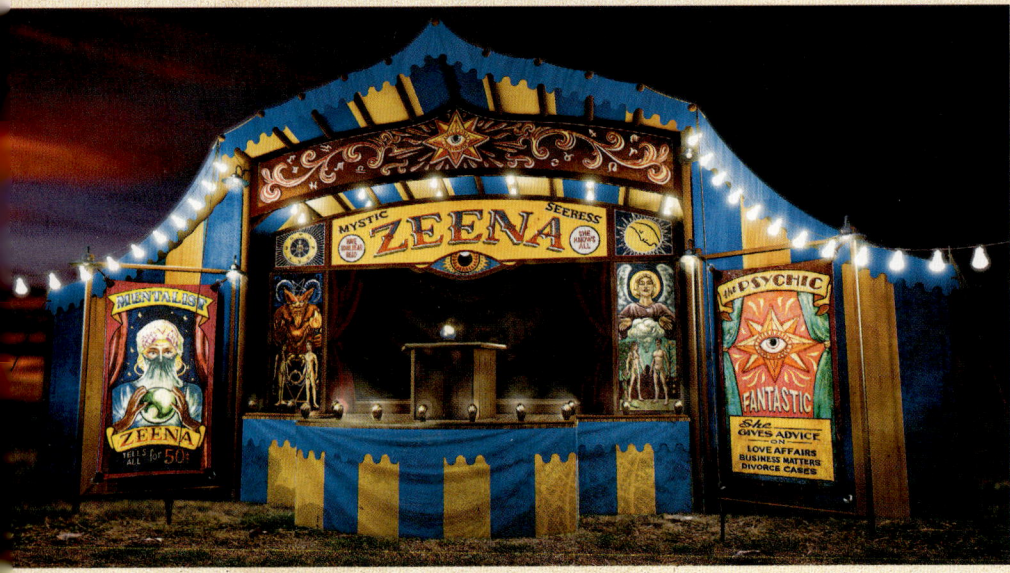

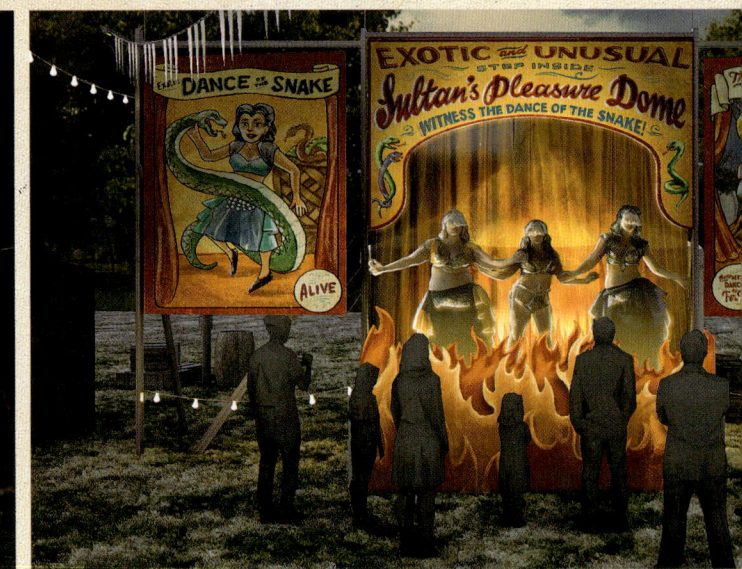

**ABOVE** A concept image shows rain falling over the carnival's covered dining tent on a moonlit night.
**LEFT** A trio of concept renderings show different aspects of the carnival: the stage where Zeena the Seer performs, the Sultan's Pleasure Dome stage where dancers entertain the crowd, and an overhead view of the carnival's layout.

collection of rides, games, stages, and other attractions she and del Toro envisioned. Their plan included a Ferris wheel, bumper cars, a carousel, and an elaborate heaven-and-hell-themed fun house, along with the sideshow tent Clem manages, which houses the pit where the geek performs.

"The carnival set was gorgeously evocative," says Zeena actress Toni Collette. "It was a living, breathing carnival. I was in awe of its pure beauty and period-specific wonder. When Guillermo first told me the story of *Nightmare Alley*, *this* is what I imagined."

**THESE PAGES** Concept artist Guy Davis spearheaded the details of the devilish design for the carnival's saints-and-sinners-themed fun house.

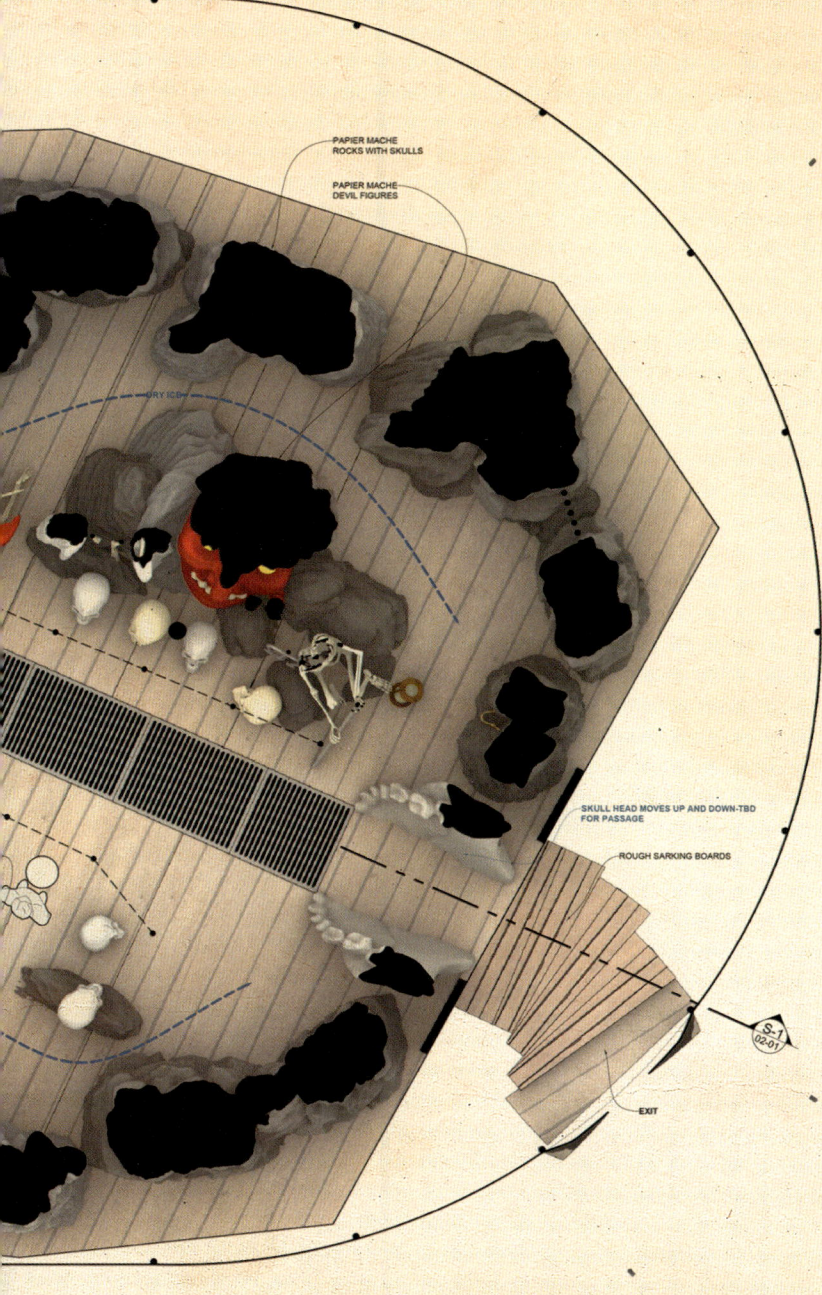

**TOP LEFT** An aerial view of the carnival layout created by Tamara Deverell's production design department.
**LEFT** An illustration detailing the interior of the fun house.
**RIGHT** (top to bottom) Guillermo del Toro and other crew members prepare to shoot a night scene outside the fun house; Clem (Willem Dafoe) tempts carnival-goers with an unforgettable show; standing beside the carnival's carousel, del Toro (far left) directs stars Rooney Mara and Bradley Cooper; del Toro inspects the fun house set.

## BANNER DAYS AHEAD

As the search got underway for a site large enough to host the sprawling carnival, the production team began to create all the props that would flesh out the detailed sets and bring them to life. "The carnival prizes, the popcorn bags, the balloons, the darts, the rings for the ring toss, everything was period," del Toro says. "The napkins for the hot dogs. The cutlery for the workers, everything."

Deverell tasked graphic artist Andy Tsang with drawing and lettering the hundreds of hanging banners that would be required to dress the carnival set. To gain a better understanding of imagery from the period, Tsang turned to reference books, including 1995's *Freaks, Geeks and Strange Girls: Sideshow Banners of the Great American Midway*. A collection of essays and archival photography depicting circus banners and sideshow acts, the book became an important resource. Prominent banner artists J. Sigler, Snap Wyatt, and Fred G. Johnson also inspired Tsang's approach.

"I took the characters in our carnival and found similar images of carnival acts—like a strongman or an elastic man," Tsang says. "I would take different elements that I'd found in that book and paint our characters in that style. I tried to make them look like the actual *Nightmare Alley* actors even though back then, when these painters

**ABOVE** The fun house ticket booth invites patrons to "enter hell."
**RIGHT AND OPPOSITE TOP** Banners and an interior design by Guy Davis for a carnival attraction based on the seven deadly sins.

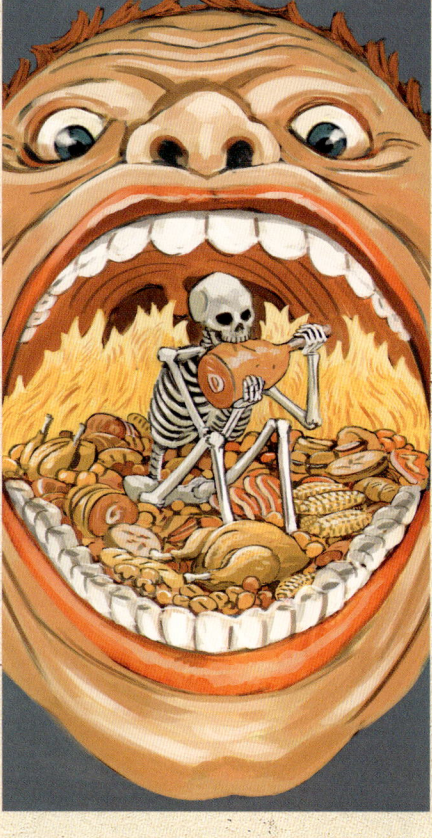

were painting banners, they didn't look like the actual people doing the acts. For movie purposes, we thought it might be good to have it look like them."

Once the banners were printed on raw muslin and grommets were added so they could be hung up on set, the banners were aged to appear dirty and worn. In fact, everything associated with the carnival was eventually aged and weathered to reinforce the idea that its glory days were long gone.

This same aesthetic was also applied to the carnival characters' wardrobe to indicate that the performers were past the prime of their careers, barely making ends meet. "It's a carnival that time has forgotten," says costume designer Luis Sequeira. "Everything is very worn out. We're

**ABOVE** Graphic artist Andy Tsang took inspiration for the banners from classic carnival images dating to the turn of the century.
**RIGHT** Carnival operator Fun House Jack (Clifton Collins Jr.) strums his guitar and sings, entertaining Molly (Rooney Mara) while Stan (Bradley Cooper) listens in.
**OPPOSITE** Additional banners created by Tsang for the film.

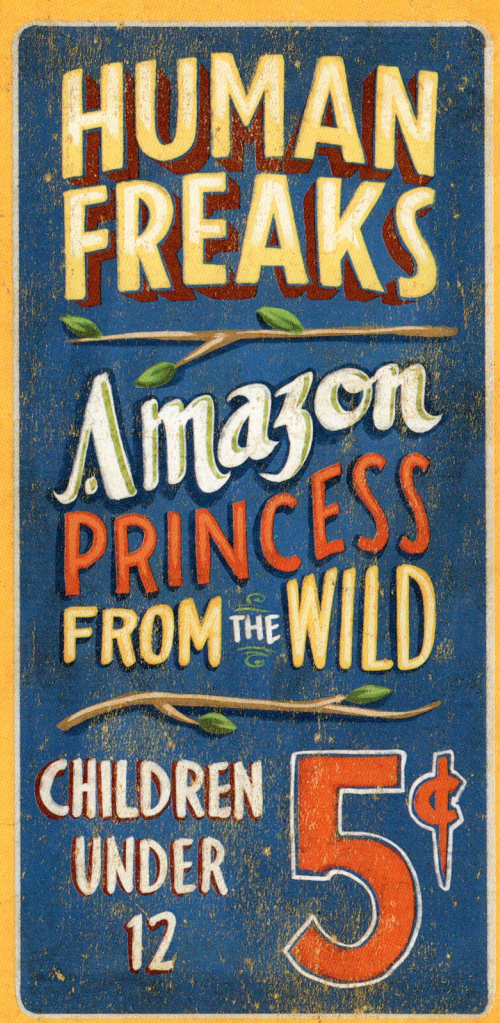

dealing with post-Depression America. Most of these people had had it quite sweet prior to the Depression, and they are still trying to still [dig] themselves out."

As he had for *The Shape of Water*, Sequeira and his team designed and created virtually all the period wardrobe and accessories for the principal members of the film's sizable ensemble. Hats, coats, suits, shirts, ties, shoes, and jewelry were all custom-made. "I would say about 90 percent was fabricated because clothing from that era is just not around, and the perfect garment for the character and the right size is not necessarily going to be there," Sequeira says.

The carnival performance costumes were "quick-on, quick-off" so that the characters could throw them over their street clothes at a moment's notice. "The idea was they would be tending to a separate part of the carnival and would then have to go perform," Sequeira says. "We did wraps and snap-backs and tiebacks for a few of the characters to re-emphasize that carnival feel. So someone could be wearing a T-shirt yet throw on a fake-front shirt that was just tied at the back."

**OPPOSITE** A banner advertising one of the carnival's more unique attractions.
**CLOCKWISE FROM TOP LEFT** Costume designer Luis Sequeira maintained a library of fabrics that he utilized for the film's wardrobe; Sequeira's rendering of Ron Perlman wearing his Bruno the Strongman outfit; Sequeira removing one of Rooney Mara's costumes from the dress form.

# FREAKS AND GEEKS

Of the many films and television series that have been set under the big top or have explored the sideshow milieu, for del Toro, there is one definitive masterwork: Tod Browning's controversial 1932 film *Freaks*. The movie served as something of a North Star for the writer-director in the unflinching way it depicts the daily realities of life for its performers. "If anyone has ever portrayed a carnival the right way, it's Tod Browning, because he knew the carnival world—he knew it intimately," del Toro says. "There is a particular cruelty to the way he portrays the carnival, nevertheless. He's not romanticizing it. He's not making it a magical world."

The follow-up to the filmmaker's 1931 classic, *Dracula*, the pre-Code horror film follows beautiful trapeze artist Cleopatra (Olga Baclanova) as she plots to marry the wealthy Hans (Harry Earles) and steal his fortune. After their wedding, she begins brazenly flaunting her affair with strongman Hercules (Henry Victor), openly humiliating her new husband, a man of short stature. Heartbroken by Cleopatra's treachery, Hans and the other performers devise shocking punishments for both his bride and her lover.

The film's cast included many real-life sideshow performers. Among them were conjoined twins Daisy and Violet Hilton; Schlitzie, who suffered from a birth defect known as microcephaly, which causes infants to be born with small heads and underdeveloped brains; and Minnie Woolsey, a woman with Seckel syndrome, a rare disorder that causes dwarfism, microcephaly, and skeletal abnormalities. Woolsey, who was also bald, visually impaired, and had no teeth, took the stage name Koo-Koo the Bird Girl.

**PAGE 92** Stan (Bradley Cooper) catches his first glimpse of the geek show.
**PAGES 92–93** A concept illustration of Stan standing beside the circular geek enclosure.
**ABOVE** Stan (Cooper) prepares a feast for the geek.
**OPPOSITE TOP** Clem (Willem Dafoe) ratchets up excitement for the gruesome performance.
**OPPOSITE BOTTOM** A detail of the banner advertising the geek show.

Browning had traveled with a carnival in his youth and took pains to include scenes in the film that showcased the members of the troupe in a positive light. Nevertheless, *Freaks* was regarded at the time of its release as distasteful and offensive and effectively ended the director's career. Del Toro is among those cineastes who view the film as revolutionary and groundbreaking. "Tod Browning has an incredibly nonjudgmental and, in my opinion, nonexploitative view of the carnival," del Toro says. "That is my opinion. A lot of people feel the other way. I think you know where his allegiance is in a movie like *Freaks*. He's certainly not aligning himself with normalcy. He's aligning himself with the outcasts."

In fact, the filmmaker is such an aficionado of Browning's film that he commissioned life-size replicas of three of its characters for his personal collection: Schlitzie, Hans, and Johnny Eck, billed in *Freaks* as the "half-boy," a performer born without the lower half of his torso. They were created by del Toro's longtime friend and collaborator Mike Hill, the English-born, Los Angeles–based sculptor who notably designed the amphibian man for *The Shape of Water* and applied much of the movie's creature makeup. Del Toro also hired Hill as a special makeup effects artist on the 2019 horror film he produced, *Scary Stories to Tell in the Dark*—and later brought him in to work on *Nightmare Alley*.

For del Toro, Browning was particularly inspirational when it came to imbuing *Nightmare Alley*'s carnival world with the right balance between "interesting and crude. The common mistake is to try to make the carnival surreal. You don't want to make it sophisticated. You don't want to make it quirky. It was an extremely rigid line in art-directing this."

With the goal of creating a well-worn, patchwork world, production designer Deverell ultimately chose to build *Nightmare Alley*'s carnival about an hour outside Toronto at Canada's Markham Fairgrounds. The site typically hosts Canada's largest annual fair

in early fall, but because of COVID-19 restrictions, the four-day event had been canceled. That gave Deverell free rein to transform an empty parking lot into a 1939 carnival.

"We picked it because it was a good, flat piece of ground," Deverell says. "It was a grassy field with gravelly areas where the cars would drive. It was level, it was dry. They had a giant horse shed that our painters could use—all our banners were aged there. They had an area where we could park our picture cars [the vintage 1920s and '30s vehicles featured in the film]. Logistically, practically, it worked well."

Deverell ordered between thirty and forty custom tents from Armbruster Manufacturing Company, the oldest tentmaker in the United States, which her art department then dyed so some would have yellow stripes and others red. The color scheme for the location hewed closely to the palette that had been established at the start of the design process, with warm earthy colors, olives, and, most important, red, a color strongly associated with the carnival environments.

For the space where the geek would perform, the behind-the-scenes team dug a circular pit in the ground. "Guillermo and I had this whole circle theme in our minds, so the geek pit was always going to be round," Deverell says. "Guillermo wanted people to just walk in and look down

**OPPOSITE** Paul Anderson, famed for his role in the UK drama *Peaky Blinders*, "threw himself into the role of the geek with complete passion," del Toro says.
**CLOCKWISE FROM TOP LEFT**, Anderson gets ready to film a scene; a sketch of the geek from Stan's notebook; the wounded geek (Anderson) lies in his cell after a failed escape attempt.

into the pit." The pit was surrounded by a circular platform lined with railings—the idea was that spectators might lean against the railings as they cast their eyes downward for the show. For scenes that couldn't be captured on location, Deverell's team built a replica of the geek-pit set on the production's soundstages.

When del Toro was looking to cast an actor to play the geek, Bradley Cooper suggested Paul Anderson. Although he had had a small part in Alejandro González Iñárritu's Oscar-winning drama *The Revenant*, Anderson is perhaps best known for his starring role as unstable British gangster Arthur Shelby in the popular crime series *Peaky Blinders*. "Obviously, we needed somebody that with literally one line would transmit the tragedy, the downfall of this character—that would break your heart with one look," del Toro says.

Although the filmmaker was familiar with Anderson's work, he was concerned that the actor was much too well established to take on a role with barely any dialogue, let alone one that would require such an enormous physical commitment. In the script, the geek is forced to lie at the bottom of a pit—even in the rain—dressed in a simple tank top and dirty, torn trousers, his long hair unkempt and covered in filth. The role also required Anderson to contort his body, either crouching like an animal or slamming himself against the bars of a cage.

Nevertheless, Anderson agreed to play the part. "Paul not only said yes but threw himself into the role of the geek with complete passion," del Toro says. "I have to be honest, I was expecting him at many points to say to me, 'What the hell are we doing? Why am I in the rain?' He never did."

"It was really miserable conditions for him because it's quite cold, and he's not dressed very well and we're getting rained on," Dafoe says. "It wasn't comfortable. What I can say about him is, he was a trouper. He also, I think, enjoyed the physicality of it because that's basically what the role is. In the story, I have to brutalize him a little bit, and I didn't enjoy that. But that's my job."

To be clear, no animals were harmed for the film—Mr. X created CG snakes and fowl for the geek show: "When the geek chases and grabs the chicken and bites into it, that's a digital chicken spraying arterial blood," Berardi says.

# ENOCH, THE LITTLE PICKLED GOD

Under the tent that's adjacent to the geek pit sit shelves of "pickled punks"—preserved fetuses that each display some terrible deformity, such as two heads or three legs. Among them is the cyclops child Enoch, who becomes a central, mythic figure in *Nightmare Alley*. The prop created for the film was modeled on a real baby preserved in a museum near del Toro's hometown of Guadalajara, Mexico, though that infant is not a cyclops.

"The rest of the body and the face are based on that baby because that baby looked almost like a very regal, godlike, above-it-all little guy," del Toro says. "He had a very wise, aloof expression, like a little pickled god. Enoch, to me, watches over the whole story. I don't know why, honestly. I just felt it in my gut that I needed him as a witness to everything."

Having worked so closely with artist Mike Hill over the years, he turned to him once again for Enoch. In the early months of 2020, the pair traveled to Mexico to view the baby that had captured del Toro's imagination. Hill then designed a model that was roughly twenty inches tall, eight inches taller than the real-life reference. "Enoch, as in the script, had lived a while after he was born, so it wasn't like he was a newborn," Hill says.

After casting Enoch in silicone, Hill added human hair to the baby's head and jagged surgical scars across the character's body, which gave him an even more unsettling appearance. Finally, he painted his creation so it would appear drained of color, like a cadaver.

"Pickled punks in real life are very pale," Hill says. "They were floating in an amber-colored liquid, so when I

**ABOVE** A concept art rendering of the sideshow tent where the numerous "pickled punks" that Clem has collected are displayed for public viewing.
**OPPOSITE** A page from Guillermo del Toro's personal notebooks depicts an early concept for Enoch.

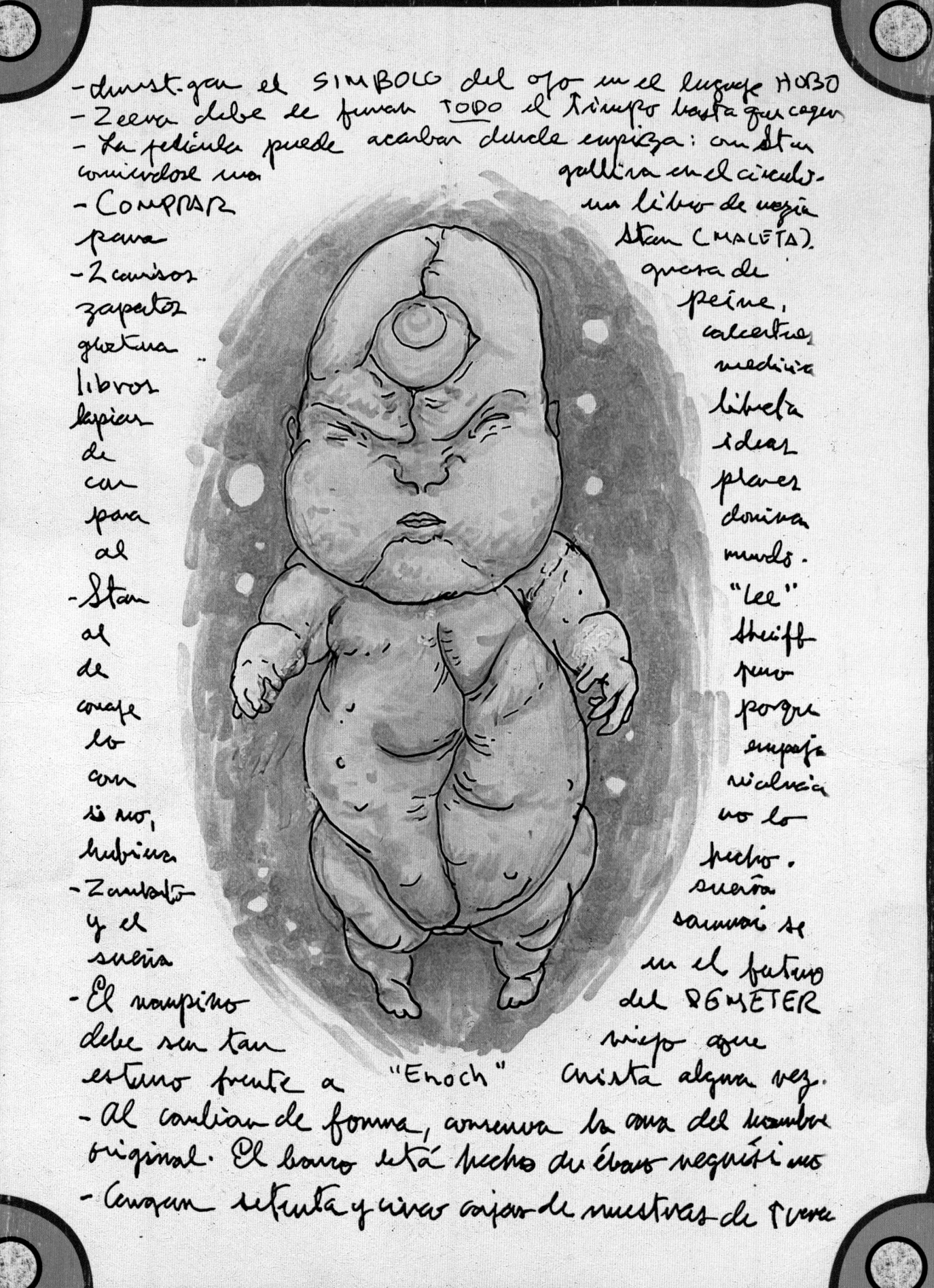

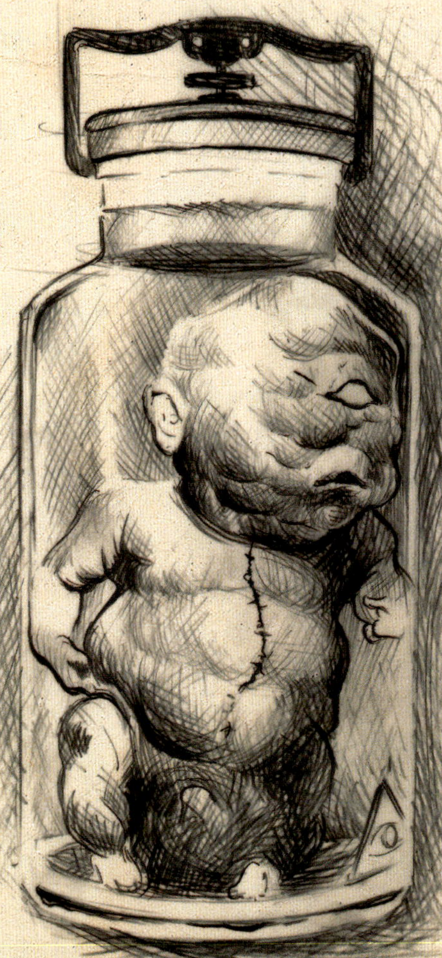

painted my little silicone statues, I would basically dip them in an amber liquid and photograph them to make sure the colors [would still look right] when we got to set. [I used] very undead colors, for want of a better term. Very jaundiced."

Working with his special makeup effects partner Megan Many, Hill also created other pickled punks for display in the sideshow. One had several legs and earned the nickname "Tripod." Another, dubbed "The Kid," had features that recalled those of a young goat. Spanish special effects studio DDT SFX was also brought in to fabricate a large number of special pickled specimens, duplicating them for background and foreground use. DDT worked on del Toro's 2001 Gothic horror classic *The Devil's Backbone*, memorably creating jarred fetuses for that film, their work on *Nightmare Alley* an oblique nod to their shared history with the director.

For del Toro, the creations took him back to his youth. Although he never witnessed a geek show as a child, del Toro did sometimes visit carnivals that weren't far removed from the one Clem operates in *Nightmare Alley*. In fact, he modeled the movie's Spider-Woman character after a performer he'd seen as a boy. "The carnivals in Mexico, when I was a kid in the '60s, they might as well have been in the '30s or '40s," he says. "They had a four-headed lamb or the Spider-Woman, the pickled punks in jars—they figure prominently in my movies because of that."

**CLOCKWISE FROM TOP LEFT** Pencil sketches of Enoch from Stan's notebook; artist Mike Hill created the life-size Enoch figure, which was then placed in a jar of amber liquid; Clem (Willem Dafoe) introduces Stan (Bradley Cooper) to Enoch; a still photograph from the *Nightmare Alley* set showcasing the "pickled punks" arranged on shelves designed by Tamara Deverell and her team.

**CLOCKWISE FROM TOP LEFT** Pencil sketch of the electric chair from Stan's notebook; a computer rendering of Molly's initial stage layout featuring twin Tesla coils; local lawmen threaten to shut down the carnival just as The Major (Mark Povinelli) and Molly (Rooney Mara) are set to debut her new and improved act; detail of the Elektra carnival banner; Molly (Mara) sits in the electric chair as Stan (Cooper) rehearses with a masked Major (Povinelli).

# THE ELECTRIC LADY

Although there's plenty of horror on offer at the carnival, there's great beauty as well, embodied most overtly in alluring performer Molly, whose porcelain skin, dark eyes, and knowing demeanor captivate Stan from the moment he first sees her. As a seasoned carny, she's got a way with audiences, too, offering up high-voltage thrills with an act that sends currents of electricity coursing through her body.

Performing on a simple wooden stage under the moniker "Elektra," she stands between two cylindrical Tesla coils, placing her hands in such a way to channel the current generated by the devices. Despite the seemingly dangerous nature of the act, Molly remains entirely unharmed. Stan, for one, is mesmerized.

Although Molly's offstage costumes are modest and typical of a young woman in the late 1930s, when she's onstage she wears a revealing dark red costume. "Her performance outfit had sequins with a gold lamé undertone," Sequeira says. "It was a two-piece outfit that back in the day was very risqué. To our modern eyes, not so much. With that, I had a silk robe that she would use to cover up when she came off the stage." A metallic hairnet completed the ensemble.

To simulate the electrical charges, cinematographer Laustsen set up strobe lights on the stage and filmed Mara acting as though waves of electricity were arcing around her body. Then, Mr. X created a digital double that they integrated into the footage and used a program called Houdini to animate the electricity enveloping her body.

"Those are maybe some of our most sophisticated effects in the film, and maybe the only time where they're kind of effects-y looking by definition," says visual effects supervisor Dennis Berardi. "Guillermo wanted the arcing to be dimensionally wrapping around her limbs, her torso, her neck, and then dissipate into her outfit. He also wanted it to look painful, so this enveloping effect was something that we had to get right in 3D. I couldn't do a 'cheap and cheerful' 2D overlay or anything like that—which you never can do on any Guillermo movie any way."

# STORMY WEATHER

When filming began after the COVID-19 hiatus, it was early October 2020—essentially half a year after the carnival sequences initially were meant to have been shot. During the long break, safety protocols had been designed to protect everyone on set. Under the new rules, COVID tests were conducted daily, masks were mandatory, and social distancing was enforced to the greatest degree possible. The protocols were so strict that the background actors who were brought in to play the carnival crowds were all required to quarantine at a nearby hotel. None were allowed to go anywhere but the film set for the roughly five weeks it took to shoot the carnival sequences.

Rather than the warm and pleasant sun-kissed days and cool nights of springtime, the cast and crew found themselves working in uncomfortably cold temperatures—often overnight—on the carnival set constructed at Markham Fairgrounds. Stormy conditions, with winds exceeding thirty-five miles an hour, sometimes threatened to damage the painstakingly designed tents and attractions.

"The weather would come up in this place and rip through it," Deverell says. "When that happened, we had to take down the banners and roll up the sides of the tents [to prevent them from being damaged]—so all of our set dressing was exposed . . . It was really like working in a carnival." Adds del Toro: "Those were sets we art-directed to a tee, but you had to contend with the fact that some nights, after we wrapped, hurricane-level winds would come in and destroy the set. When the winds came, twenty-five prizes would blow a mile and a half away, or one of the tents would be in the next county the next morning."

Together, the wind and rain could make for a chilly, soggy set, and when shooting at night, it was almost always difficult to remain warm. "It was late fall in Toronto, so it was cold, and it was damp, and it was a challenge," says Bruno actor Ron Perlman. "But these are things one does when one makes a movie."

A veteran of multiple del Toro productions, Perlman felt the tattered, threadbare nature of the carnival was an intriguing artistic choice for the filmmaker. "This set was deliberately dingy and dusty," Perlman says. "Old tired billboards, old tired stages—you could tell there was a tremendous amount of wear and tear. It was a departure from the beautiful worlds Guillermo usually traffics in, which have all this elegance and opulence to juxtapose against the detritus that lurks underneath. In this case, the detritus was worn onscreen."

"It's really his most naturalistic movie," adds producer Dale, whose professional partnership with del Toro dates to *Mama*, the 2013 horror film they produced together. "Normally with him, there are going to be a lot more allegorical parallels, metaphors in his work, more fantasy or heightened reality. The naturalism of the story and the environment is not something he's ever done before really. He lives in a world of monsters and dream creatures, but I think he's showing his range here."

That isn't to say, of course, that monsters aren't lurking in *Nightmare Alley*'s darkest corners. Stan engages in all sorts of monstrous behavior before leaving the carnival behind. He fleeces Zeena out of the mind-reading act that once made her and her husband, Pete, famous. And in a terrible mishap, he fatally poisons Pete after giving him a bottle of wood alcohol instead of the booze he'd requested—though Pete isn't the first person to die by Stan's hand. "All the males in the movie are possibilities of what Stan could be," del Toro says. "His father, Pete, Clem. There are three father figures, basically. He kills two of them."

It's another death, however, that marks the end of Stan's initial carnival days. After Stan narrowly averts a catastrophic encounter with a local lawman who wants to shut down the carnival (played by *Crimson Peak* actor Jim Beaver), the performers hold an impromptu celebration. But their evening of revelry soon takes a tragic turn when Clem and Louise's child is delivered stillborn. "You could milk the hell out of that because it's a big moment in the story, at least for the carnival characters," Dafoe says. "You don't want to back away from it, but you want to be very careful with it and give it the same kind of reality that you give the other things. I think we kept it very simple."

The next morning, the world looks different—the landscape is drained of color. Deciding the time has arrived to embark on a new life together, Stan and Molly load up a truck with their belongings and begin driving toward an unknown future. Meanwhile, the all-seeing eye of Enoch looks on.

**OPPOSITE** Death comes to the carnival as a distraught Zeena (Toni Collette) cries out in grief after the body of her husband Pete (David Strathairn) is discovered.
**RIGHT** Clem (Willem Dafoe) cradles the body of his stillborn infant.

# CHAPTER FOUR
# RESURRECTION OF THE DEAD

*At the call of an angel with fiery wings, graves open, coffins burst, and the dead are naked.*

**Worlds away from the grit and grime of the carnival circuit, the gleaming upstate New York metropolis of Buffalo stands as a jewel of art deco architecture, flush with old money and hungry for entertainment. It's there that Stan reinvents himself as a master mentalist gifted with tremendous psychic ability. Performing the same routine that Pete and Zeena had perfected decades before, Stan and Molly are the headlining act at the chic Copacabana nightclub.**

Despite his newfound success, Stan is perpetually restless and dissatisfied, convinced that he must be destined for yet greater things. As he rubs elbows with the city's elite, he doesn't realize that he's wildly out of his depth. Naively assuming they will be as easy to manipulate as the rubes who turned up to gawk at the circus acts, Stan will miscalculate in ways that cost him dearly.

"This world is much colder and harsher than Stan is prepared for," del Toro says. "Stan is a big fish at the carnival. He's like a barracuda. Everybody else is a lot more permeable and malleable and painfully human. But in the city, Stan is an amateur. Stan is a little barracuda in a city of sharks."

To emphasize the idea that Stan is unknowingly imprisoned by his metropolitan surroundings, del Toro and production designer Tamara Deverell supplanted the earthy, organic spaces and wide-open skies of the carnival world with a collection of claustrophobic corridors, imposing edifices, and sleek interior spaces. Colder colors become dominant, with greens, ivory, black, and gold the most prominent hues.

Red is almost entirely absent. "The only reds in the city are on Molly," del Toro says. "There are no reds in the city, no reds in the streets, no reds on the extras. All the red, all the life, stayed in the carnival—quite literally, the last thing you see as Stan leaves the carnival is a red balloon lost in the middle of the sky."

The filmmaker also utilized sound design to amplify that sense of confinement. "Every door that opens and closes in the city opens and closes with [the sound of] a hermetic seal," del Toro says. "Even if it's wood, it opens and closes like a seal. The few doors that are in the carnival creak and moan. You feel the wood and the rust. In the carnival, Stan is free—there's the sky, the air. He didn't want that. He wanted more."

**BELOW** Molly (Rooney Mara) wears her red dress coat and hat as she heads to a Buffalo office building on an important errand.
**OPPOSITE** "Luis [Sequeira] did such a beautiful job," says Mara of the film's costume designer. "The costumes always help take you there."

# DESTINATION BUFFALO

When del Toro and co-screenwriter Kim Morgan were working on the *Nightmare Alley* screenplay, they chose Buffalo as a principal location for several reasons. In 1941, the city was still at the height of its grandeur as both an industrial powerhouse and a cultural hub. The successful Pierce-Arrow Motor Car Company, which manufactured luxury cars and commercial trucks from 1901 to 1938, had brought prestige, as well as an influx of cash, to the area. Dignitaries would routinely visit Buffalo—authors Mark Twain and F. Scott Fitzgerald both had ties to the city, which was also renowned for a thriving nightlife scene.

Still, the city has rarely been seen onscreen. Del Toro had set part of *Crimson Peak* there, but all the Buffalo scenes were filmed on location in Toronto. "Buffalo had so much wealth at one point, and some of that old wealth stayed there—incredible wealth [was concentrated] in a few hands," del Toro says. "We thought that was more interesting than going to any of the cliché big cities [like] Chicago, New York. Then

**OPPOSITE** An ominous night sky looms over the Buffalo bus station in this concept image.
**BELOW** Concept art of the interior of the bus station.

**BELOW** The unclaimed property room Stan visits looking for important clues to Grindle's past was created on location in Buffalo and closely corresponded to these two early concept renderings of the set.
**OPPOSITE** Bradley Cooper in costume as Stanton Carlisle during location shooting inside Buffalo's majestic City Hall.

you have to re-create landmarks that don't look the same at all. The Copa in Buffalo never existed, but you can create it."

Buffalo can also lay claim to a distinguished architectural tradition, with such celebrated talents as Frank Lloyd Wright having designed buildings there. In addition, the city is home to a number of impressive examples of art deco architecture. The style came to prominence in France in the 1920s and gained popularity in America in the ensuing decades with its geometric patterns and its use of glossy materials, such as mirrors and chrome. Buffalo has gone to great lengths to preserve that storied history, with many of its most beautiful buildings looking much as they did when they were constructed.

"It's almost like an architectural catalog of American buildings," del Toro says. "It has exquisite art deco buildings, particularly the government buildings. They have Edwardian and Victorian houses that are fantastic. There are a couple of neighborhoods that are entirely 1800s houses. You can go to Buffalo and find an entire [century-old] courtroom or an entire meeting hall that is preserved."

Filming for four days in Buffalo during the terribly cold February of 2020, the production visited various sites centered on the area of Niagara Square, including City Hall. "Within a ten-block radius, there are just some jaw-dropping buildings," says producer J. Miles Dale. "But it was a brutal four days. If you watch the dailies, you'll see people not moving their feet, and they are still moving. They're being blown by the wind across an icy sidewalk."

Although the buildings in Buffalo look much as they did in the early 1940s, life around them has moved on—meaning that the scenes shot on location in the city needed to be digitally altered to remove any trace of the modern world. Dennis Berardi and his team at Mr. X handled the augmentations while also adding subtle period details to some of the exterior scenes. "Basically, every time you see an exterior, we will have shot it on a location, but then we'll have replaced anything that looks modern with our digital period assets that we created," he says. "We've got dozens of period extras in different costumes that we can employ in any shot. We've got vehicles that we've created digitally that we can put in—different colors, taxicabs, trucks."

## INSIDE STAN'S NEW WORLD

**Although the wintry city streets provide a breathtaking backdrop for *Nightmare Alley*'s second half, most of the Buffalo sequences take place inside luxuriously appointed rooms within the city—among them the Copacabana stage, the dressing room Stan shares with Molly, and the hotel suite where the couple reside. Deverell designed every space to include the bold lines and geometric patterns so strongly associated with the art deco movement, though circles take on special significance.**

Del Toro wanted Stan to be surrounded by circles wherever he goes. Although he might not notice their presence, the shapes ominously recall the carnival's geek pit. "There is not a single straight corner in the city if we can avoid it," del Toro says. "Most of the corners are rounded. I wanted Stan to be surrounded and trapped. The club is circular. His dressing room is all rounded like an oval."

For the Copacabana, Deverell initially planned to re-create a previously existing set she'd designed for *The Strain*, which had been modeled after the Round Room at Toronto's historic venue the Carlu. Built in 1930, the Carlu's Round Room is a striking space with impressive circular moldings set into its domed ceiling. Del Toro had been so taken with Deverell's original set that he'd repurposed it for *The Shape of Water*, which was shot at the same soundstage facility where the action-horror series was filmed. In the Oscar-winning movie, it doubled as the Black Sea Russian Restaurant, where a plot unfolds to kidnap the film's amphibian man from the facility where he's being held captive.

With *The Strain* having completed its run and that original set no

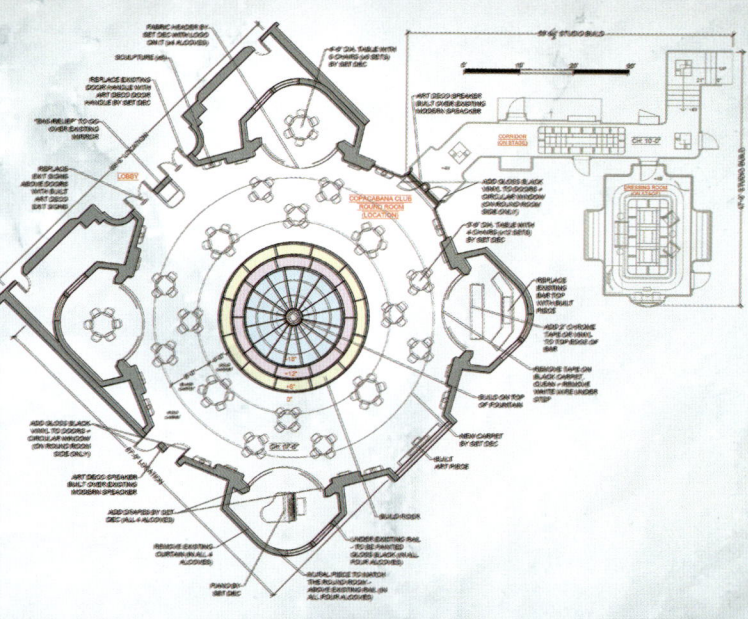

**CLOCKWISE FROM TOP LEFT** A rendering of the dressing room that Stan and Molly share shows the beautifully appointed space with its circular mirror and window; the circle motif resurfaces in a rendering of the Copacabana performance space where Stan entertains the well-to-do; the film's circular motif is again visible on this schematic showing the layout of the Copacabana set; a rendering of the Copacabana corridor highlights the sleek lines and bold colors strongly associated with the art deco movement.

**OPPOSITE** Bradley Cooper, Cate Blanchett, and Rooney Mara film the confrontational scene in which Lilith interrupts Stan's show at the Copacabana, leaving Molly unsure what to do.
**ABOVE** Backstage at the Copa, Stan (Cooper) attempts to reassure an unhappy Molly (Mara).
**BELOW** The blindfold Stan (Cooper) wears during his performances is adorned with a single, staring eye that recalls the watchful spirit of Enoch.

longer standing, del Toro asked Deverell to build a new and slightly more expansive version on the production's soundstages. Given the costs involved, however, it was more prudent to simply shoot the Copacabana scenes on location in the real Round Room at the Carlu. There was just one problem: The beautifully detailed ceiling that del Toro wanted to feature so prominently was too high. If he were attempting to film Stan and Molly performing beneath the dome, the details of the ceiling would remain out of frame. Deverell came up with a solution.

"I proposed to Guillermo that instead of lowering the ceiling, which we obviously couldn't do, we'd raise the actors," Deverell says. "We ended up building another round element, this giant gloss-black dais for Molly and Stan to be on while they were performing. It worked beautifully in this space."

In contrast, both Stan and Molly's dressing room and the hotel

suite they share were built on soundstages. The latter was based on one of the bedrooms at the lavish Parkwood Estate in Oshawa, Ontario. Inspired by early twentieth century Beaux-Arts design, the lavish 15,000-square-foot, 55-room mansion now operates as a museum offering tours of its impressive interiors and the breathtaking landscaped gardens.

Although Stan lives and works in these places, notably he's not truly at home in any of them. "I didn't really think about his character in terms of making a space his," Deverell says. "Even his father's country shack where he grew up was not his space. I think that's part of his character. He never belonged. He never felt the love that he wanted as a child. He's a misfit. Nowhere feels right."

In keeping with the newer, more elegant environments, costume designer Luis Sequeira upgraded the wardrobe for Bradley Cooper and Rooney Mara to reflect their characters' new place in society. "When we move to the city, everything for Stan is brand-new," Sequeira says. "The clothing is pristine, well pressed, and well tailored. There's quite a jump in aesthetic and cut and fit to the costumes. The fabrics are luxe. There's a little tinge of new money, a nouveau riche quality to things. Stan is accessorized to a tee. Generally, he's pretty spiffy."

Viewing Molly essentially as one of his most important accessories,

**CLOCKWISE FROM TOP LEFT** Concept art for the lobby of the hotel that Stan and Molly call home; an artist's rendering of the entrance to the historic hotel; concept art showing more of the handsome brick building; Rooney Mara films a scene in which Molly checks in at the front desk.

Stan buys her a closet full of beautiful gowns that reflect the height of 1941 style. "Stan wants to keep up with the Joneses, so she has a lot of really lovely dresses that she wears in the city," Sequeira says.

Most of the characters in Buffalo—including Stan—wear cool-toned monochromatic costumes made from oyster, black, and navy fabrics, but Sequeira made sure to include red in Molly's costumes to emphasize her strong ties to the carnival. One of her most stunning pieces is a full-length black velvet evening gown adorned with a red butterfly motif. "It looks like there was a kaleidoscope of butterflies flying around the dress," Sequeira says.

**CLOCKWISE FROM TOP LEFT** An elaborate tapestry hangs over Stan and Molly's circular bed in this rendering of their hotel suite; in the warm light of dawn, circles dominate the hotel suite while Molly (Rooney Mara) and Stan (Bradley Cooper) go about their morning routine; Toni Collette and Mara, in costume as Zeena and Molly, seated on the rounded green sofa within the hotel suite set; Stan (Cooper) turns on the charm for Molly (Mara) while she sits in front of the room's circular dressing mirror; filming the hotel reunion sequence in which Molly (Mara) is happily reunited with The Major (Mark Povinelli) and Bruno (Ron Perlman).

## LILITH MAKES AN IMPRESSION

As lovely Molly as might be, Stan is nevertheless drawn to enigmatic psychiatrist Lilith Ritter. They meet at the Copacabana when Lilith interrupts the duo's nightclub act, insisting that Stan intuit the contents of her handbag. Later, she explains she was merely testing the veracity of Stan's gifts at the behest of local magistrate Judge Kimball and his wife (played by Peter MacNeill and Mary Steenburgen). The grief-stricken Kimballs desperately want Stan to serve as a conduit that will allow them to speak to their dead son. Instantly infatuated with the coolly perceptive blond, Stan agrees to help the couple, over Molly's strenuous objections.

Lilith also proves too tempting for Stan to resist. She effortlessly radiates all the qualities Stan works so hard to project, exuding wealth and sophistication. To design the character's glamorous evening wear, Sequeira drew inspiration from screen sirens including Greta Garbo and Joan Crawford, designing expensive velvet gowns for her in gray and gold.

"She was of old money, and so we really utilized beautiful fabrics that had some form of texture and reflective quality because of the low-light [environments]," he says. "It was important for me to give her a luster and then impeccable tailoring. We had a cape dress made of two-toned velvet in gray and amber with the underlining of it in a copper or warm gold. There was another velvet dress that had copper appliqué stitched into the velvet. That was an off-the-shoulder dress with a bustle and a train. With that was this beautiful velvet cape with gold embellishments at the shoulder."

When Stan goes to see Lilith at her office during daylight hours, he arrives to find her looking equally stunning. In one instance, she wears a black suit that pairs a shawl-collared jacket with an A-line skirt that hugs the curves of her body, creating a silhouette reminiscent of a cello. "Her suits were very distinctive, had some sheen, and each of them had a distinct color," Sequeira says.

"Luis is a master of texture and detail," says Lilith

**OPPOSITE** Cate Blanchett as Lilith on the well-appointed office set created for her character.
**ABOVE** The expansive Lilith's office set featured inlaid wood paneling, stained glass windows and skylight, as well as custom furniture designed and fabricated by Tamara Deverell and her team.

actress Cate Blanchett of the costume designer. "He built it from the underwear up. How the costume felt was as important as how it looked which was not an experience I've ever had with a designer."

If Lilith's refined wardrobe speaks to her wealth, her office is on another order entirely. With nearly every scene between Lilith and Stan playing out within the confines of this intimate space, del Toro and Deverell wanted to create an opulent environment that felt removed from the outside world.

"Their entire relationship takes place in Dr. Lilith Ritter's office, and we thought about that space as being a psychological space," says Blanchett. "In a way, it was the space where Stan was most exposed and vulnerable. I kept thinking about Lilith and Stan's relationship as being a little bit like a dance of death. There's a lot of destructive urges in all the characters, definitely in Stan, but I think in parallel in Lilith. There's a lot of darkness there and a lot of damage beneath what seems to be a quite pristine exterior."

Deverell modeled the office on the Weil-Worgelt Study, an art deco masterpiece designed by Parisian decorating firm Alavoine sometime between 1928 and 1930. On display at the Brooklyn Museum, the study features geometric paneling of palisander and olive wood veneers and a small bar concealed in a corner closet; at the time the study was constructed, Prohibition was the law of the land. Still, says Deverell, "The study in the Brooklyn Museum is tiny compared to what we ended up building."

Standing roughly forty feet long and eighteen feet wide, the set for Lilith's office grew to include a working fireplace and a side table with four chairs at the entrance to the room, in addition to her desk and her green velvet psychiatrist's sofa. There was a vintage bar cart, too, a piece that was not only an attractive adornment for the set but also a narrative requirement. Every time Stan visits Lilith, she pours him a glass of whiskey—even after he tells her he never drinks. As their relationship evolves, though, he begins to develop a taste for alcohol, one that quickly becomes all-consuming.

"We got some beautiful art deco furniture from all over the world and re-covered it, but some of the pieces we just had to make," Deverell says. "We built a sitting table, and the sofa she has in front of the window. We based the sofa off an existing art deco piece that we had reference images of. It was very plush and seductive."

The office also featured custom built-in bookshelves, sliding doors, and wood paneling inlaid with a subtle Rorschach-test pattern. "The organic wood grain patterns hit such a good note for somebody who's a psychiatrist and for such a stark geometric space," Deverell says.

To finish the set, Deverell gave the office a coffered ceiling and a high-gloss marble floor. "It was really a knockout set—just the shine of it, the intensity of the wood," she says. "All the wood was heavily shellacked, which is what they did in those art deco environments at the time. It's very much trying to take a powerful woman who's smarter than smart and make this office that is almost glowing around her. It was full of wood and warmth and shine and exemplified strength and power—female power in particular."

Although she is not personally an enthusiast of the deco movement, Blanchett describes the set as a "marvel." "I understood Lilith from the inside out simply by standing in the space," she says. "It's hard to articulate except to say the office was a living, breathing Rorschach test. I felt there was blood behind those walnut-paneled walls."

**OPPOSITE TOP** Guillermo del Toro directs Bradley Cooper and Cate Blanchett on the Lilith's office set.
**OPPOSITE CENTER** Stan (Cooper) tries to impress Lilith (Blanchett).
**OPPOSITE BOTTOM LEFT** Del Toro (left) supervises a scene on the Lilith's office set.
**BELOW** Lilith (Blanchett) perches on the green velvet couch in her psychiatrist's office.

# STAN VS. THE MACHINE

The lengthy conversations between Lilith and Stan begin as a sort of flirtatious verbal sparring before evolving into a full-fledged affair, but there's always something darker and more fraught at the heart of the lovers' interactions. As she studies Stan's vulnerabilities, Lilith also appeals to his innate greed with a scheme to pry millions from businessman Ezra Grindle by exploiting a tragedy from his past. Although Grindle is hardly an easy mark, Lilith is always quick to offer Stan a drink to calm his rattled nerves.

Stan's first encounter with the titan of industry becomes a true test of his con man skills. The reclusive Grindle insists that Stan come to his offices, where he must take a lie detector test to prove he can commune with the dead. "In the book, Stan is tested by a machine built by Grindle, but a true explanation of the 'how he did it' is never really offered, not in a satisfactory way," del Toro says. "So, Kim and I decided that a lie detector, which was a nascent

**BELOW** A Guy Davis concept for the lie detector machine.
**RIGHT** Richard Jenkins's Grindle (left) watches as Stan (Bradley Cooper) attempts to pass a lie detector test.

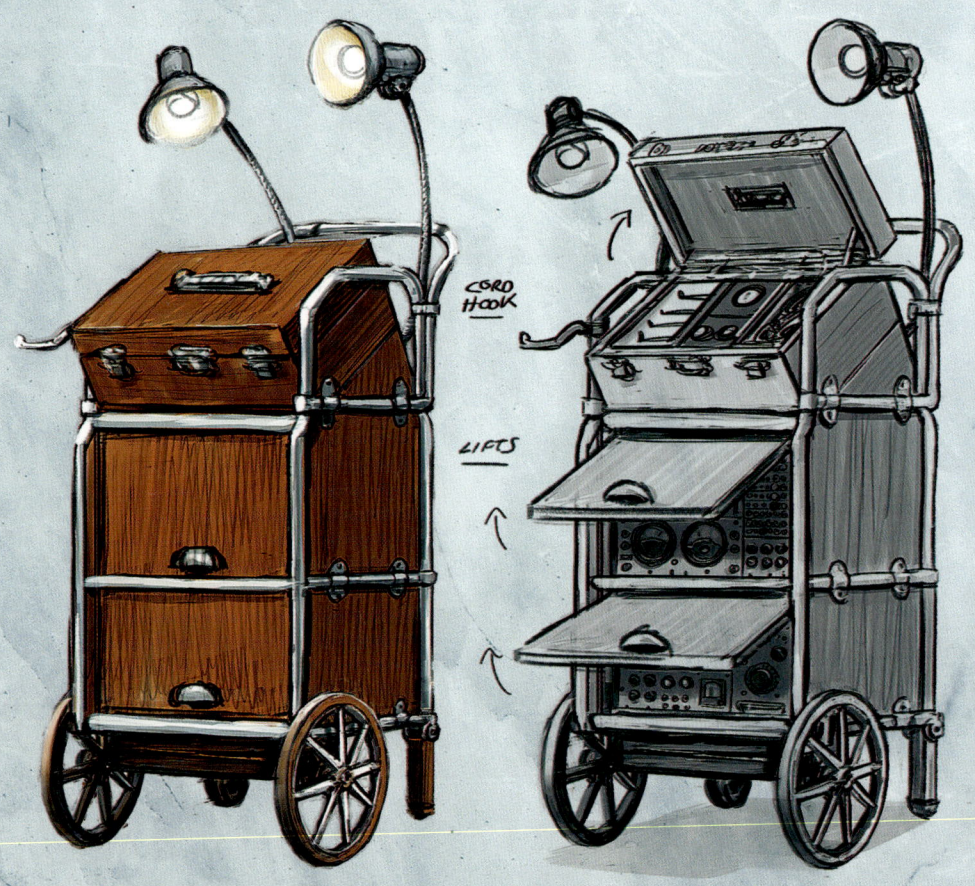

technology at the time, would be a perfect substitute."

Calibrating the tension in the lie detector scene was particularly challenging, del Toro says. "We need to know he's lying, but no one else in the frame can know he's lying," says the filmmaker. "Oh my god, those [distinctions] are hard to gradate, I cannot tell you.

"Some of the performances [in my films] are beautiful and stylized, but those are the ones that I needed to resist on this movie," del Toro continues. "For example, I'd ask Bradley to lean closer to the lens, and we would do it and it would look *fantastic*. But earlier takes than that revealed a greater degree of truth, so we'd go for the not-so-showy take. Does he look like he's really speaking to the dead? Or does he look like a really good performer in 1941? If he looks like he's speaking to the dead, that's the take."

**CLOCKWISE FROM LEFT** This rendering depicts Stan and Anderson arriving at the lobby of Grindle's imposing offices and checking in at an enormous circular desk; a concept image shows a repeating pattern of circles inlaid on the floor of the offices; a detailed render of the lobby desk includes sleek geometric accents.

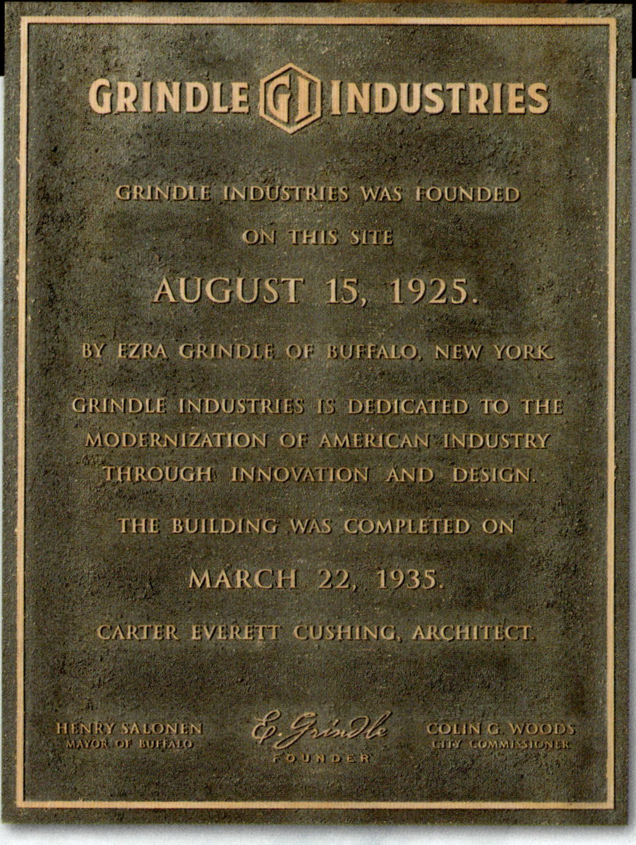

To navigate that high-wire act performance, Cooper would meet with del Toro every day, two to three hours before cameras would roll, to discuss each upcoming scene in detail. "We would take everything that we would have been preparing in terms of character and dynamics and we would flay it open," del Toro says. "Then, when we got to the location or the set, we would be very fast. Very fast, very furious."

Jenkins notes that the relationship between filmmaker and star was seamless. "He and Guillermo collaborated beautifully," says Jenkins. "Bradley would sit next to Guillermo and look at the cuts of the takes. There's no ego with Bradley. The only thing he's interested in is the best film he can make. He roots for you. He's a genuinely giving man who wants this to be the best movie we can make. And he's a wonderful director, too."

**CLOCKWISE FROM TOP LEFT** This rendering shows Stan and Grindle amid the sumptuous trappings of the magnate's office decor; a concept depicts the interior of Grindle's mansion; a bronze plaque commemorating the founding of Grindle Industries used to dress the exterior location at Scarborough, Ontario's R. C. Harris Water Treatment Plant; concepts for an intricate four-panel mural created by production designer Tamara Deverell to adorn the walls of Grindle's offices.

To make Grindle appear even more imposing, Deverell created an office for the character that in some ways was the larger and more masculine counterpart to Lilith's. The exterior of Scarborough, Ontario's R. C. Harris Water Treatment Plant served as the facade for the building where he works, while the interior was constructed onstage.

"[The interior set is] this vast open space with these three huge chandelier lights that we built from scratch," Deverell says. "It's much more monumental and monolithic than Lilith's, with high ceilings, stone floors, and stone walls. His fireplace was all black marble. We did a lot of sculpted bronze inlaid pieces behind his desk in this central hall when you come in. Grindle's supposed to be this rich, rich man."

**OPPOSITE TOP LEFT** A concept illustration shows the exterior of Grindle's offices at sunset.
**OPPOSITE TOP RIGHT** Concept art depicting the millionaire's lavish estate as seen from the vantage point of the property's sprawling gardens.
**BELOW** Surrounded by grassy lawns, the R. C. Harris Water Treatment Plant is an art deco landmark and made an ideal location for the production.

**LEFT** Stan observes Grindle's many tributes to his late lover, Dorrie, in this rendering of the lavish private gardens Grindle constructed in her memory.
**OPPOSITE** Grindle (Richard Jenkins) and Stan (Bradley Cooper) stroll through the gardens; these scenes were filmed on location at the historic Parkwood Estate.

# THE GHOST OF "DORRIE"

**Against all odds, Stan ingratiates himself with the older man, serving as his highly paid spiritual adviser and storing his ill-gotten gains at Lilith's office. As far as Stan is concerned, when the con is complete, he and Lilith will leave Buffalo to begin a new life together. Stan feels he has no reason to mistrust the psychiatrist. He's shared some of his darkest secrets with her—and in an intimate moment, she, too, has opened up to him, unbuttoning her blouse to reveal the jagged surgical scar that runs down her torso. Notably, it echoes the scar on the body of little Enoch, the carnival god.**

The idea for the disfigurement was one that originated with Blanchett herself. "I thought if there was . . . some physical damage that went along with her that belied this beautiful exterior, that that would be quite an interesting duality to play with," she says. "It came out of discussions with Guillermo—*What if it was from some terrible accident that we never find out about?* It's a way of genuinely exposing herself to Stan as he exposes himself to her, his fear and his failings. It also is a physical way of saying without words that this world is incredibly dangerous and no one can exist without damage being caused to them."

Del Toro was careful to preserve the mystery around not just Lilith's background, but the other major characters' as well—including Stan's. Although he filmed flashback scenes to Stan's younger days that shed light on his psychology, he chose not to include them in the final cut. "The thing is," says del Toro, "the more you explain something, the more it diminishes."

Grindle buys Stan out of his contract at the Copa so that the mentalist can come to work with him full-time. But Grindle becomes increasingly impatient with his new employee and demands that Stan materialize the spirit of Dorrie, his lost love. Realizing that he needs to find a way to deliver, Stan devises a scheme in which Molly, dressed in a wig and an old-fashioned white gown, will pretend to be the spirit of Dorrie.

For the "Dorrie dress," costume designer Luis Sequeira created a long-sleeved diaphanous white-on-white organza gown with a basket-weave front and a striped skirt. "It was really a play on see-through but not," Sequeira says. "We aged it and did an ombré of a slight lilac tone to give it a bit of a base so it's not just a floating thing. It has some grounding to it. It gives it more dimension."

Even though Molly knows that Stan's plan is both morally wrong and quite likely to go awry, she allows him to cajole her into participating. "We talked a lot about that—why does she go?" Mara says. "I think Molly really truly is a diehard romantic and sacrifices herself for the ones that she loves, which is why she goes in there. Part of that is so beautiful, to not give up on someone. She really believes in Stanton and really believes in the goodness of people and wants to keep giving people chances—there's something really beautiful about that."

When Grindle embraces "Dorrie" and begins to run his hands over her body, Molly breaks character

**OPPOSITE** Soaked in theatrical blood, "Dorrie" (Rooney Mara) arrives in Grindle's garden.
**ABOVE** An early concept by Guy Davis shows a naked "Dorrie" on the grounds of Grindle's mansion.
**RIGHT** Molly (Mara) comes face-to-face with a stunned Grindle (Richard Jenkins).

and calls out for Stan. At that moment, the ruse is over. "Why she can't go through with it ultimately is because she does have a moral compass, unlike most of the other people around her," Mara says.

For Jenkins, the scene was an especially memorable one to shoot. "There was a line I ad-libbed, and we kept it," he says. "I grabbed her legs, and I'm telling her, 'I'm sorry. I'm sorry. Forgive me.' Then she says, 'I can't do this anymore.' I stand up and I look at her, and I say, 'Who are you?' We had all kinds of conversations around, 'What do we say here? What's the line?' I just thought, 'Who are you?' was probably as good as any. Then Bradley beats me to death."

**OPPOSITE** Stan (Bradley Cooper) attacks Grindle (Richard Jenkins) as Molly (Rooney Mara) attempts to escape.
**ABOVE** Molly (Mara) flees for her safety.
**LEFT** Wrapped warm against the frigid nighttime temperatures, Güillermo del Toro works with costume designer Luis Sequeira.

## STAN'S DOWNFALL

After Grindle calls out for his bodyguard, Anderson, Stan panics and begins pummeling his mark, both out of sheer rage and to ensure that Grindle will be unable to report his crimes. Cooper, Jenkins, and del Toro worked out the choreography for the fight on set, but Jenkins says the physical acting required was relatively limited. "Bradley's a big strong guy, and I'm an old guy," Jenkins says. "Two punches, and I'm dead on the ground. It was basically him hitting me really hard, breaking my jaw probably, breaking my neck. It looked like an overmatch between him and me. That's the thing that made it brutal."

Although del Toro is typically a strong proponent of using practical makeup effects, for *Nightmare Alley*, the fatal injuries sustained by Grindle—and, subsequently, Anderson, who dies when Stan runs him over with his car—were all created digitally, owing to the complicated nature of the scenes as well as to COVID-19 safety precautions.

"The gruesome moments in *Nightmare* are moments that you cannot repeat easily," del Toro says. "So I decided to take what we learned about digital and try to apply it. We thought that was the only way to go, and creatively, it fit."

Grindle's wounds were therefore rendered by the team at Mr. X, who replaced Jenkins's face with their digital version. "Stan basically crushes Grindle's nose in, right down to pulp," Berardi says. They also created a digital double for Anderson during the hit-and-run scene. "It's a digital car, digital actor," Berardi says. "Then, in the aftermath, Guillermo wanted to have a flap of Anderson's head almost plop down, like a toupee that flops down, with blood pouring out into a cone in the snow. It's quite a dramatic scene."

That terrible act is the last straw for Molly, who resolves to leave Stan and move on with her life. Realizing he needs to skip town immediately, Stan goes to retrieve the money he's stashed at Lilith's office, only to learn to his great surprise that she's betrayed him to the authorities and taken his loot. "The fatal mistake Stan makes is he thinks money will give him power, but in fact, it's power that gives you money," Blanchett says. "The people who are pulling the strings will always be pulling the strings."

The discovery sends him into a spiral from which he'll never recover. "She beats him at his own game," del Toro says. "She's not out to swindle Stan, but she may use the money to teach him a lesson . . . He thinks he's the same class intellectually as Lilith. He thinks he's a super smart guy,

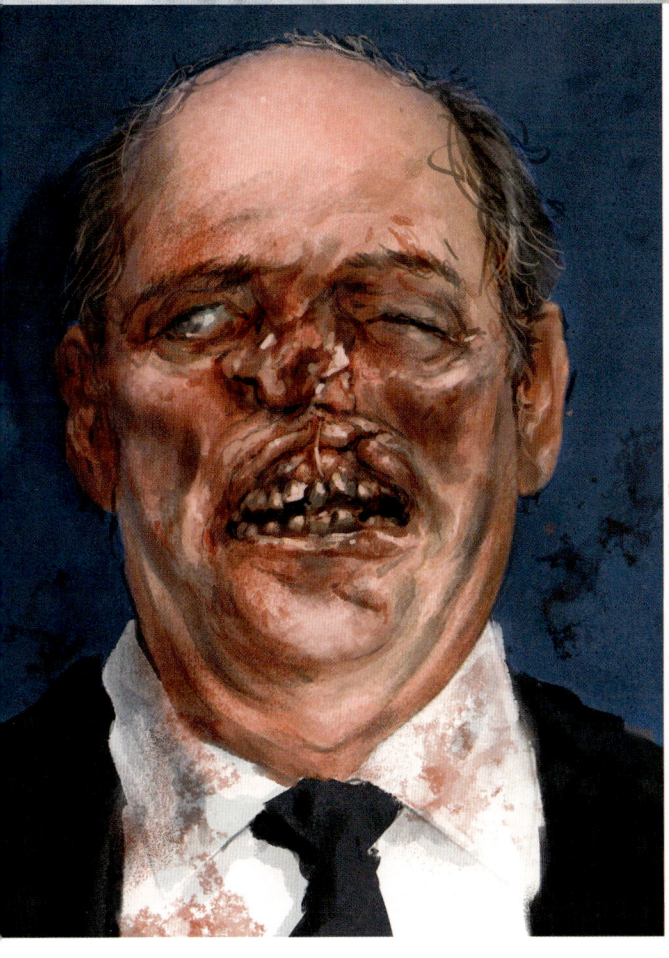

and she tells him, 'You're nothing but an Okie with straight teeth.'

"Ultimately, I think Lilith is almost an avenging angel to all the things that Stan does through the movie," del Toro continues. "In the movie, everybody ends alone, so to speak. You imagine very clearly that Molly will go back and be part of that [carnival] family again. You imagine that Zeena will be alright. And very pointedly, we have what for me is a great line—Someone asks Lilith, 'Are you okay?' and she says, 'I'll live.' I think that's the main thing. All these characters will survive this guy, this swindler, this dark dreamer, a dark seeker—but he will not."

**OPPOSITE** Stan's final confrontation with Lilith (Cate Blanchett) turns violent.
**ABOVE** A concept by Guy Davis details Grindle's mangled face.
**RIGHT** Guy Davis storyboards depict Anderson's violent death.
**FAR RIGHT** Realizing he's been betrayed, Stan (Cooper) flees through the streets of Buffalo.

## CHAPTER FIVE
# THE HANGED MAN

*Hangs head downward from the living wood.*

From the outset of the project, screenwriters Guillermo del Toro and Kim Morgan knew that they wanted the film to maintain a fealty to William Lindsay Gresham's novel and the staggering bleakness of its finale. "The book ends with a punch in the face," del Toro says. So when their adaptation concludes, Stanton Carlisle, now a full-blown alcoholic, has nowhere left to turn, no one left to swindle, no one left to love him. And as fate would have it, after living in a homeless encampment, he finds himself under the big top once again.

But compared to Clem's operation, the outfit that Stan stumbles across, Amberson Carnival, is far shabbier and more sordid. There's not much in the way of work on offer, especially for a guy like Stan, who, after months on the run, turns up at the manager's office smelling of urine and booze. There, he's stunned to see his old portable radio perched on a shelf. Enoch, the cyclops god, is there, too, peering out at him from his jar of formaldehyde. "The symmetry of the movie is [that] we finish the way we open, and we make it circular in some ways, like a nightmare," del Toro says.

Shaken, Stan nevertheless attempts to pitch his old mentalism act to the boss, but the carny manager, played by award-winning actor Tim Blake Nelson, quickly shoos him away. But as Stan turns to go, the boss suddenly has a change of heart. There *is* one job open. Maybe Stan would be willing to fill in? Just until they find a new full-time geek. It's a proposition Stan grimly accepts, saying simply, "Mister, I was born for it."

"It's a sad thing to say," Morgan says. "Carnies are made, they're not born. He's saying this is who he is. It's sad that you would think you were born for that. It's tragic that he thinks that. But there's some acceptance, too."

**OPPOSITE TOP** Concept art depicting the hobo encampment that Stan temporarily calls home.
**ABOVE** Tim Blake Nelson plays the operator of the Amberson Carnival.
**LEFT** Blue is the dominant color in this artist's rendering of one of the Amberson transport vehicles; the cool hue stands in contrast to the vibrant reds that were so prevalent at Clem's carnival.

**TOP** A digital rendering of the entrance gate to the Amberson Carnival. The banner at the top right advertising "Chang & Peng" is a reference to Chang and Eng Bunker, conjoined twin brothers who gained fame in the nineteenth century.
**ABOVE** A further rendering shows an alternate view of the Amberson Carnival midway, which was far more modest than the film's principal carnival.
**OPPOSITE** At rock bottom, Stan (Bradley Cooper) goes to see the Amberson Carnival manager about a job.

The exact wording of Stan's last line was the subject of great debate for Morgan and del Toro: Should Stan say that he was "born" to be the geek? Or should he say he was "made" to be the geek? "We had huge symposiums about the last line," del Toro says. "The difference was immense. Ultimately, 'born for it' prevailed. It's a destiny that has chased him since he was a kid. The [reason the] movie is completely pregnant with circles [is] because the destiny of Stan is the arena of the geek, which is a circle. I think that the notion of destiny is a chain of decisions that something very dark and unexamined in you makes. But it's a series of decisions of which you are the actor."

The Amberson Carnival scenes were shot at the same location as the film's primary carnival, Markham Fairgrounds. But unlike the earlier carnival, Amberson had none of the convivial atmosphere that brought the first location to life. Whereas hay and mud provided ground cover for Clem's carnival, Amberson tents sat atop dust and sand, recalling the Dust Bowl. "The carnival at the end of the movie has a very different vibe," Deverell says. "We built it within our carnival, we used a lot of the same elements, but we completely denuded all the sets and all the banners. We made a very desaturated, nicotine-stained world for that one."

Del Toro decided that the final scene inside the carny boss's office would include "everything that defines Stan and that he has been avoiding—the circle, the red," the filmmaker says. "[The set had] this almost uterine texture, very organic, very womblike. He goes into a red space, and he cannot escape anymore."

**OPPOSITE LEFT** Gripped by alcoholism, a disheveled Stan (Bradley Cooper) is a shadow of his former self.
**OPPOSITE BOTTOM RIGHT** Wearing masks, Guillermo del Toro and Cooper confer during filming of the Amberson Carnival scenes.
**ABOVE** Enoch is prominently displayed in this rendering of the Amberson Carnival manager's office.
**LEFT** The Amberson Carnival was constructed on the same location as *Nightmare Alley*'s primary carnival, Canada's Markham Fairgrounds.

# AMBERSON'S TEN IN ONE
## "HUMAN FREAKS AND LIVING WONDERS"

## ON WITH THE SIDESHOW

The film's final moments also gave del Toro an opportunity to briefly pay tribute to Tod Browning's *Freaks*. To emphasize the down-and-out nature of the carnival where Stan's story ends, he decided that one of the acts would be a sideshow with performers based on two specific players from the 1930s movie, Koo-Koo the Bird Girl and Schlitzie. Although his *Nightmare Alley* characters closely resemble Browning's, they have different names.

"You see Fee Fee the Bird Girl and you see Zizi for a second," del Toro says. "Originally, it was all over the script, and I said, 'No, that's going to be distracting. I don't want the movie to be an appendix to *Freaks* or a footnote to *Freaks*. It needs to have a different feeling.' But if you read the story of carnivals, the smaller and less prestigious carnivals got, the more they carried freaks, even when they were outlawed in many states by that time. This is not a great carnival. It's a dingy carnival."

As del Toro was working in Toronto, he gave special makeup effects supervisor Mike Hill license to cast Los Angeles–based actors to play both Fee Fee the Bird Girl and Zizi. Having someone local was

**PAGES 150–151** Stan arrives at Amberson Carnival in this evocative concept piece.
**TOP** A banner rendering for Amberson Carnival.
**ABOVE** An early sketch for a Zizi banner.
**OPPOSITE** Zizi was played by actress Samantha Rhodes, who spent roughly three hours in the makeup chair before arriving on set.

important for Hill because he planned to refine the character makeup before arriving on the *Nightmare Alley* set. (Hill donned prosthetic makeup himself to appear in the film briefly as Jojo the Dog Boy.)

Relative newcomer Samantha Rhodes was cast as Zizi; Dian Bachar, an actor who has had small roles in such films as *Galaxy Quest* and *The Adventures of Rocky & Bullwinkle*, played Fee Fee. Rhodes's makeup took roughly three hours to apply and included a prosthetic neck appliance, a nose and upper lip, a brow piece, ears, and then a point for the top of her head. "The trick for Zizi is to try to enlarge everything else and leave the top of the head small," Hill says. "We enlarged the nose and the chin and the teeth and the neck and made the ears bigger. Things like spacing the eyebrows out differently than they typically are on the human head [helps]."

All the prosthetics were cast from silicone rubber and painted before they were applied to Rhodes's body, as were the full rubber sleeves she wore, which were covered with fine hairs to give her a more masculine appearance. "The whole point was to make the character seem like this androgynous person," Hill says.

Rhodes shaved off her long black hair for the role. "She was a really amazing sport," Hill says. "I didn't want to put a bald cap on her because hiding her hair would have added bulk, and we couldn't do that. So one

**LEFT** Jojo the Dog Boy—played by lead artist and special effects makeup designer Mike Hill—frightens carnival patrons with his stage performance. "I designed a color pattern for the hair that started darker on the mane," Hill says. "The cheeks were lighter, and the nose was almost blonde."
**ABOVE** Key artist and special effects makeup supervisor Megan Many applies Hill's Dog Boy prosthetics.

**TOP** Mike Hill pulls rubber sleeves over Zizi actress Samantha Rhodes's arms; the prosthetic pieces were designed to give Rhodes's character a more masculine appearance.
**ABOVE LEFT** Rhodes is further prepped for shooting.
**ABOVE RIGHT** Hill looks on as Guillermo del Toro makes adjustments to Fee Fee, played by Dian Bachar.
**OPPOSITE** Carnival banners advertising Amberson sideshow attractions.

stipulation for this character was that the actor would be willing to shave her head. I couldn't watch the first bit being cut. She didn't care. She loved it. She loves her hair short now, but I, as the person who asked for that, felt very bad about it."

For Bachar's transformation into Fee Fee, Hill completely covered the actor's body with six large silicone appliances. Only his eyes were visible, though Bachar wore special glasses to make them appear larger. For both characters, Hill referred to old carnival photos rather than looking to Browning's film for inspiration, and made a point of learning about the physical ailments that had afflicted the real-life performers.

"When you're doing any of these characters, it doesn't matter if you're doing a fantasy creature such as a werewolf, you still go and study lycanthropy," Hill says. "You still go and study wolves. It's all part of the big picture to absorb yourself in these images."

# A DARK PARABLE FOR TROUBLED TIMES

**In many ways, the homage to *Freaks* is fitting. Del Toro's *Nightmare Alley* has an emotional wallop similar to that of Browning's film, with a protagonist facing a comeuppance so extreme that it becomes pitiable. Stanton Carlisle is more multifaceted than the gold-digging Cleopatra in the earlier movie, however. He can be malevolent, yes, but he's also lost, adrift, with no moral compass and no tools to bring to heel his worst instincts. "In the book and what we did, it's not written in a way to punish anybody," Morgan says.**

As an insightful character study, though, *Nightmare Alley* offers a powerful reminder that with every choice in life come inescapable consequences. "One of the themes that Guillermo has talked about is that no man can outrun himself," says producer J. Miles Dale. "Ultimately, if your intentions are not honorable, you will find your way to demise. Stan tries to remake himself and takes what might otherwise be noble aspirations, and he chases them down a dark alley. He chooses the wrong path."

The film also very intentionally speaks to the terrible toll deceptions can take on both the individual who obfuscates the truth and anyone unlucky enough to fall for the con. "We exist in a world where you can construct ten separate sets of realities with the same information assembled in different narratives," del Toro says. "If everybody can believe everything about anybody, if anything can be true, if there's no objective truth, it's extremely scary."

Artistically, *Nightmare Alley* represents a new high-water mark in del Toro's already remarkable career. It's a deeply felt, psychologically gripping drama that centers on one dark soul and the complicated characters who exist in his orbit—a tale that might be fairly described as painfully human. For the filmmaker's close friend and frequent collaborator Ron Perlman, it serves as yet another testament to del Toro's singular creative vision and his continued evolution as a cinematic storyteller.

"In terms of the pantheon of Guillermo's work, this is a departure on a lot of different levels, but it's almost *more* Guillermo than we've ever seen before," Perlman says. "He's a once-in-a-generation kind of guy. He was born to be a filmmaker and has the eye of a Picasso or a Rembrandt and the sensibility of the most interesting writers you could ever imagine reading. I knew it from the minute I met him and particularly from the first frames of *Cronos* . . . His frames contained real artful compositions and so much evocation and energy. He goes into that very, very small handful of guys who shook the world cinematically."

For del Toro, *Nightmare Alley* is a clear expression of his personal preoccupations at a moment of incredible cultural tumult. The film, with all its dark imagery and harrowing themes, offers a clear window into the present state of his psyche.

"I jokingly say that if I'm lucky, when people see everything I've done, they will have an idea of what's in my library at my house," del Toro says. "I've been able to express the manga of it all with *Pacific Rim*. I've been able to express my affinity for Victorian gothic romances with *Crimson Peak*. I've been able to express my love for Mexican literature through, strangely enough, *The Devil's Backbone*, and so on.

"I had made *The Shape of Water* as a love song," he continues. "I found such harshness in the world that I couldn't make a whimsical movie, at least not for the moment. I don't know if I'm ever going to make another one that is whimsical. The whimsy was squeezed out by reality in the last few years. For me, the carnival and *Nightmare Alley* is where I am. I feel that the themes that are in that movie are the themes that are alive in my head right now. This is how I feel. And that's all I can do with my movies, express how I feel. Because for me, the movies are not a filmography. They're a biography."

**OPPOSITE** *Nightmare Alley* filmmaker Guillermo del Toro.
**LEFT** The cast and crew of *Nightmare Alley* pose for a group shot on location at Markham Fairgrounds.

# Titan Books

144 Southwark Street
London SE1 0UP

www.titanbooks.com

Find us on Facebook: www.facebook.com/titanbooks
Follow us on Twitter: @TitanBooks

© 2021 20th Century Studios.

All Rights Reserved. Published by Titan Books, London, in 2021.

No part of this publication may be reproduced, stored in a retrieval system, or transmitted, in any form or by any means without the prior written permission of the publisher, nor be otherwise circulated in any form of binding or cover other than that in which it is published and without a similar condition being imposed on the subsequent purchaser.

A CIP catalogue record for this title is available from the British Library.

ISBN: 978-1-78909-881-5

Publisher: Raoul Goff
VP of Licensing and Partnerships: Vanessa Lopez
VP of Creative: Chrissy Kwasnik
VP of Manufacturing: Alix Nicholaeff
Editorial Director: Vicki Jaeger
Executive Editor: Chris Prince
Editorial Assistant: Harrison Tunggal
Senior Production Editor: Elaine Ou
Senior Production Manager: Greg Steffen
Senior Production Manager, Subsidiary Rights: Lina s Palma

Designed by Amazing15

Concept art created by Guy Davis, Tamara Deverell, Chris Penna, Vicki Pui, and Andy Tsang.
Tarot card designs by Tomás Hijo.
Costume sketches by Greg Hopwood based on designs created by Luis Sequeira.
Chapter opening quotes extracted from *Nightmare Alley* by William Lindsay Gresham.

Insight Editions, in association with Roots of Peace, will plant two trees for each tree used in the manufacturing of this book. Roots of Peace is an internationally renowned humanitarian organization dedicated to eradicating land mines worldwide and converting war-torn lands into productive farms and wildlife habitats. Roots of Peace will plant two million fruit and nut trees in Afghanistan and provide farmers there with the skills and support necessary for sustainable land use.

Manufactured in Turkey by Insight Editions

10 9 8 7 6 5 4 3 2 1

# ACKNOWLEDGMENTS

**Insight Editions and the author would like to extend their deepest gratitude to Guillermo del Toro for his help and support in the creation of this book. In addition, Gary Ungar was instrumental in greasing the wheels and propelling this project forward. Special thanks also to Kim Morgan for her assistance in fact-checking the manuscript and providing additional insight into the creation of the film.**

Many thanks also to the hugely talented cast and crew, who took the time to share their insights into the process of making *Nightmare Alley*: Dennis Berardi, Cate Blanchett, Toni Collette, Willem Dafoe, J. Miles Dale, Tamara Deverell, Mike Hill, Richard Jenkins, Rooney Mara, Holt McCallany, Ron Perlman, Luis Sequeira, and Andy Tsang. Thanks, too, to the people who helped facilitate interviews about the film: Lauren Auslander, Dominic Buccieri, Frank Frattaroli, Lisa Kasteler, Graehme Morphy, Jonathan Pinzon, Rhonda Price, Hylda Queally, Christine Tripicchio, and Jen Turner. The author also wishes to personally thank George and Violet Ricker for their love and understanding—and everything, really.

Finally, thanks go to Dylan Holfus, Rachael Lyon, and Jacquelyn Silverman at Searchlight, along with Carol Roeder and Nicole Spiegel at Disney, for their enormously valuable assistance throughout the production of this book.